BEING AND CIRCUMSTANCES

Book I: Circumstantial thinking and ontological thinking

by Oscar Brenifier and Leila Millon

Book II: The imposture syndrome

by Oscar Brenifier, Kathryn Cook and Viktoria Chernenko

Editions Alcofribas

2024

Table of contents

Part I:

Circumstantial thinking and ontological thinking

Chapter 1

Circumstantial thinking

The circumstances are the conditions, events and situations connected with a phenomenon and affecting it, be it a personal action or an impersonal happening. Its etymology is Latin and comes from the verb circumstare (encircle, encompass) constructed from circum "around" and stare "stand". Therefore, it refers to external parameters or to the context affecting the cause and the form of a phenomenon, the idea of "standing"indicating a more substantial or essential feature of a phenomenon, its center of gravity, what sturdily remains. In the case of a "free subject", such as the human being, the circumstances of an action primarily refer to what is not under the dominion of this subject.

A circumstance is therefore an element or a set of elements that will condition, contextualize, modify, minimize or underline a fundamental or essential fact or event. It will determine an ambiance, an environment, a reality, producing the context in which a phenomenon occurs. The principle of circumstantial thinking is to tend to explain a situation based on external or surrounding events, that usually are not an integral part of the subject itself, but rather people, events, facts or diverse interacting factors around him, external to him. By the term subject, we mean the entity, primarily a human being, which is at the center of the issue, the main cause of the action, considered "free". The problem we then face is to determine to which extent a phenomenon is attributable to the subject itself or to those external factors. First, when we try to explain a given situation through external factors, we commonly mention the family, the education, the immediate environment, specific persons, the culture or the society as a whole, anything that can be used to describe a context. Second, the past of a person, his life story, his diverse experiences, particularly the unpleasant, difficult or traumatic ones, his habits, are also often used to account for some action or behavior, as if it were a factor external to the subject at a given moment, whereas they constitute his inner self. A third circumstantial modality is the transcendental explanation, referring to some higher power, neither controllable nor really explainable, rather mysterious and implacable, such as God, karma, fate, nature, doom, malediction, misfortune, although we claim to be able to observe its effect and impact upon the subject. Fourth, with more objective or scientific pretensions, is the personal identity of the subject, predetermined and fixed, for example his genetic inheritance, his biological or psychological characteristics, even his metaphysical nature, assigned as fundamental features of his self, in a rather essentialist perspective, since it does not allow any freedom or distance from this "nature".

A conceptual distinction that can be useful in this context is that between cause and condition. A cause is that which produces or effects a result, that from which any phenomenon actively proceeds, without which it would not exist. A condition is a circumstance, singular or plural, or a situation, which allows a phenomenon to occur, without which this phenomenon cannot occur. The cause is manifest, it effectively operates, the result is visible. The condition is latent, the phenomenon might happen or not happen, depending on other factors. The cause is necessary and sufficient, the condition is necessary but not sufficient. A crucial aspect of the difference is the unpredictability of the event: a cause is singular, it comes out of "nowhere", it can irreversibly modify the course of events, it is discontinuous, when the condition is a rather permanent phenomenon, its action is continuous, it is more predictable. De facto, in a deterministic system, there are no causes but only conditions, since there is no free determination or autonomy; we could say it is totally circumstantial, everything is explained by the context. Inversely, if circumstantial explanations tend to refer to conditions, a more conclusive form of demonstration, it can as well refer to a cause: "He forced me to do it", "This event made me angry", etc.

Referring to circumstantial elements is usually used as a way to put a particular emphasis or impart a specific angle of analysis, provide a given spin on the description and understanding of the behavior or action of a subject, explaining his way of being. It can have the effect of dramatizing a description or explanation, or on the contrary to soften or attenuate the importance and the gravity of a phenomenon, lightening its practical and moral implications. We use it to explain an observable phenomenon, especially by paying attention to its causal nature, to its genesis, to its condition of possibility and causes of occurence, as the generating process modifies the reality of a phenomenon, as it affects our perception and understanding of it. This generating process, identified and expounded, will determine the value and significance of the event, by attributing responsibility and burden to some factors of the action considered efficient or primary.

Circumstantial argumentation can be observed for example in the judiciary process, when there is a trial. The defense lawyer or the prosecutor will mention circumstances, which can be aggravating, in order to confirm the responsibility of the defendant or to obtain a stronger condamnation, or mitigating, in order to alleviate the charge or to exculpate the defendant. In this case, circumstances will be considered as objective arguments that can help the judge or the jury to render a better decision, since they can evaluate more adequately, more globally the behavior and deeds of the defendant. Thus, if the defendant had suffered from strong parental abuse, if a rapist had suffered from a rape himself, or if the defendant had no previous criminal records, those circumstances could help to reduce the gravity of the crime and invite to a reduced final sentence. While, in an opposite way, if it can be proven that he has prepared and calculated at length his crime, that his motivations were quite sordid, that he had indeed consciously and viciously intended to cause harm, those elements will tend to aggravate the sentence. The nature of the intention and the degree of consciousness or conscience are the main parameters that generally make a difference in the assessment of a demeanor. The history of the individual, his momentary mental state, his status, the behavior of his victim, be it an individual or society as a whole, the premeditation or impulsivity of the incriminated gesture, will also affect the appreciation of the situation.

In daily life, circumstances are commonly used as a reason for our actions, in particular the questionable ones, since we are generally ready to fully accept responsibility for positive deeds. And just like in the judiciary process, those circumstances are used either to disculpate ourselves – or others – from wrongdoings, diminish the blame and avoid the punishment or negative consequences that could incur from those wrongdoings. Thus, they easily and naturally become an excuse, a justification, an alibi or a claim for acquittal, for ourselves or for those we wish to protect, in order to shirk any responsibility, as a means to avoid criticism and blame. For some persons, it becomes a common way of thinking and speaking, to such an extent that even when they are not accused of anything, or when no suspicion weighs on them, they naturally tend to explain events primarily through their circumstances. It becomes a certain frame of mind, a certain style of speech, sometimes rather compulsive. Therefore, when such persons want to explain some action or event, they want to provide the listener with a profusion of details, viewing most minute elements as a necessity, indispensable in order to understand and deliver the "truth"of the situation. The global effect is often to provoke confusion, to lose the thread of the narrative or the explanation, to forget the main issue, a chaos that affects just as much speaker and listener. Although, when one wishes to defend or protect oneself, this confusion can prove itself quite efficient and useful.

The circumstances can be external, when we describe events beyond our own control as the reasons or conditions for our own actions. One can therefore conclude that we were forced into a situation for which we cannot be held responsible. Circumstances can as well be internal, when we attribute for example the cause of our actions to some fixed or established feature of our being: our nature, our essence, our genes, our culture, our education, our unconscious, etc. They can be mysterious, incomprehensible or without identifiable mechanisms, such as luck, accident, fate, etc. "I didn't do it on purpose"is a typical usage of "accident"or "unconscious"to avoid taking responsibility for our actions or to extenuate our guilt. Although one might say that internal circumstances bear a slightly more ontological component, since it is less accidental and more intrinsic than the purely external ones. "He is violent because he was not loved as a child", "He is violent because he is an angry person", "He is violent because he wants things to go his own way"represent a three-step gradation into the ontological dimension. The first one is totally external, the second is internal but general and fatalist, the third one is more specific and allows for some self-determination. Although we might add to the second type of explanation that, when applied to oneself: "I am violent because I am an angry person", it implies a dimension of consciousness and therefore a certain degree of freedom, through the distance one generates with oneself in such a declaration, which makes it rather ontological.

We should mention specifically the concept of "trauma", a serious "life accident" commonly used to explain individual actions and personality, a typical format of circumstantial thinking. We can summarize it as an external circumstance modifying in an intense and negative way the psychology of a person, transforming his being, making him generally unhappy, anxious, powerless, violent, or else. There are two ways of analyzing this issue, we could call it a choice, although it also depends on the intensity and gravity of the initial event. One is a pathological way, where the subject is a suffering victim, troubled by "unchangeable" past events. Another is an existential way, where the subject deliberately determines or modifies the narration of the event and its consequences, problematizes its analysis, expressing his fundamental personal freedom, an attitude that even questions the very concept of trauma. Obviously the probability of the first modality is strengthened by the seriousness of the initial event. Although too often in our society, where the principle of vulnerability and victimhood is somewhat glorified, the pathological reading of the "trauma" is largely favored.

Of course, as explained before, circumstances can be used to falsify the description of a situation and the personal involvement of a subject. But on the other hand, when we have to pass a judgment on someone, be it in daily life or in the judiciary process, when one has to render a sentence on the defendant or determine his degree of responsibility, we cannot ignore the numerous facts surrounding or composing the event under examination. It can definitely be useful and essential to take under consideration diverse types of elements, essential or accidental, even sometimes minimal details that can indeed make a difference. In court, in order to have a full picture and to determine, based on the law and the circumstances, what the sentencing should be, in life, in order to assess the morality or character of a given person, or evaluate a specific gesture. We can establish that it is impossible to completely ignore the "externality" of the individual reality, if only to appraise how a given individual relates to this reality, a crucial dimension of this individual's identity. Otherness is real, a subject is not alone in the world, events and situations are interconnected. There is a necessity to understand one's environment to understand him. For example, a subject who lives in the middle of the war and the other who lives in a peaceful country, will not share a similar context, won' t live in the same way, won't benefit from a similar "providence", and based on this, they won't have the same options, they won't make the same choices, they won't live the same life. Killing someone else will necessarily not have the same meaning, it will not have the same significance. Thus circumstances are not to be erased completely, as they can be part of determining the nature of the being and his behavior, we cannot ignore for example the social dimension of an individual.

We can mention here the Sartrean vision of things, according to which freedom is always "in situation", immersed in a context and limited by it. Freedom is therefore to throw oneself into the world, to lose oneself in it in an attempt to modify it, to act on it. Freedom is a void within human reality. This nothingness that is man remains an incompleteness: man remains always to be done. Freedom is absolute, insofar as it decides the meaning to be given to the constraints. His acts result from a project, from the choice that man makes of himself, by accepting that the will is not an all-powerful faculty. It has meaning only in the original project of an always intentional freedom. Freedom allows consciousness to free itself from the facticity of the given evidence of things, it founds the world and shapes it.

It is true that some given circumstances can engender psychological tensions, they can distort our behavior or blur our judgment, in a way they can alienate the authenticity of our self through the disturbance, the instability or the cognitive dissonance they provoke. People can behave in an "abnormal" way because of a certain context, and we can then explain this particular behavior through the circumstances. Some events can provoke difficulties, engender struggles, produce pressure and constraints that can neither be ignored nor erased or forgotten. For example, "I was tired", "I was in a rush", "I was angry" , "I was in pain", or even "I was drunk", different contexts described to explain the modification of our psychological state, thus qualified as accidental and out of profile. "We were not ourselves" is the hidden message, therefore we should be forgiven, "it should not count" . But there is another way to think about these "particular" situations: not as an "accident", not as "foreign", but as a "revelator" of our self. One way to justify such an interpretation is that in usual life, different mechanisms such as morality, social conventions or rationality inhibit or reduce our instinctive urges or drives. But when we are immersed in a powerful context, when we are unusually psychologically overwhelmed, these inhibiting agencies cannot function anymore, they take us by surprise or they are too powerful, allowing our "natural" self to come out and reveal itself. Thus, when we act in such a "strange" way, we can either use the circumstances as a self-sufficient explanation of the abnormality, being under constraint or duress, or we accept the hidden reality that emerges as a characteristic of our inner self, divulging and laying bare some fundamental aspect of our being.

Therefore, one has to be careful when it comes to understanding the human being, his behavior and his character, in order to determine when and how to look for profound reasons and motivations for his actions in opposition to merely observing the facts, when and how to criticize those actions, when and how to account for the context, etc. Circumstantial thinking can become a problem, as it does not focus on the essential, the crux and core of the subject. It is often mistakenly used as a reason, as a cause or as an explanation, instead of being perceived as a secondary element, as it often should be. This contextual thinking then, by focusing on the accidental, becomes a way to negate the fundamental, to divert from it or to dilute it, and so it reduces ontological thinking to a secondary or nonexistent dimension, suppressing its reality. It focuses on what can appear as a reason, based on a given context, but evading the fundamental nature of being. We could say that circumstantial reasoning is based on a sense of reduced causality, a causality that for instance identifies only the immediate event provoking some movement or action. It is for example an efficient cause instead of a final cause, a distinction made by Aristotle with his theory of "four causes": final (motivation or purpose), efficient (triggering or immediate cause), material (substance or structure) and formal (nature or essence). The efficient cause provides a quick explanation, and gets rid of the thinking process. Circumstantial explanation is a quest for immediacy and justification, often external but internal as well, which denies the responsibility and the power of a subject.

People justify themselves through circumstances, in order to minimize the gravity of their actions, or to avoid taking responsibility for a problem. It becomes a way to speak in bad faith, in order to avoid diverse problems such as confrontation, bad conscience, guilt, shame etc. By hiding behind an external context one does not deal with one' s true nature. It is indeed easier and more comfortable to blame the traffic for being late than to admit one's issue with time, space, reality or a more obvious difficulty such as procrastination. Just like it is easier and more comfortable to use one's character or nature in order to explain our action, rather than through a deliberate decision. For example, "I became angry because I have a hot temper"sounds less ridiculous than "I became angry because I wanted him to agree with me"; expounding our nature is used in this case to hide the infantile side of our desire.

Circumstances are traditionally used as a type of excuse. An excuse is a reason we give, either true or invented, appropriate or inappropriate, to explain or defend our behavior, to justify ourselves and be forgiven. In a more hypocritical way, it can be a "good"reason that we give for doing or not doing something, when our motivation is of a quite different nature. For example, when we want to refuse an unpleasant invitation, we will use the argument of lack of time, or being busy. From this standpoint, we can see that circumstances can be factual, rather objective, or can be fictitious and artificial. In a more complicated way but still common, they can be factual but used in a fictitious way, therefore producing a strong alibi. The problem is that we are not always able to clearly distinguish the subjective from the objective in our own speech, in particular when we are under the strain of justifying ourselves, when we have to worry about some punishment, deal with some tension, or simply protect our image. Very often, people will rather unconsciously use some flimsy argument to defend themselves, nevertheless expressed with a good dose of sincerity, when it is obvious for the listener that these excuses do not hold water. Although a little effort of distance and critical thinking on their part would allow them to become aware of the problem. We could add that the main difference between an excuse and a reason is that the latter includes the possibility of change, it is reasoned, it can be problematized, when the excuse, unreflective, is invoked as a fatality. Thus circumstances are often artificially fabricated, being rather shallow or illusory, but social codes generally prohibit their denunciation: expressing doubt and criticism about excuses provided to justify oneself would be considered offending, therefore it should be avoided.

The usage of circumstances can also be understood as a recourse to condition. A condition is what must exist as a fortuitous occasion, as concomitant with an event, what is required for something to happen. At the same time, it becomes an essential qualification, a necessary stipulation, it provides unavoidable specified terms without which a phenomenon will not take place, an action will not be realized. A condition is therefore some constraint on which we depend, and most of the time this condition is presented as a reality which is outside of our control, be it a concrete reality or a general one. Therefore the mention of such a condition frees us from any responsibility since it deprives us from any freedom of action. Our being becomes therefore submitted to an uncontrollable, external and powerful impediment, we become a victim, which implies that we are not accountable anymore for our own actions and behaviors.

Circumstantial thinking is quite connected to a circumstantial conception of existence, what can be called "practical life" or "survival life". People whose daily agenda is primarily characterized by an interaction with the world in order to satisfy some desires or needs, those who are strongly concerned with such an interaction, those who are permanently requesting and hoping for external gratification. Their daily existence is filled and even saturated with events that please or displease them, they constantly receive or perceive signs from the outer world, a world which primarily escapes their control, an external reality that arbitrarily determines their state of mind. Therefore, naturally, their explanations of events will be circumstantial, since the contingency of circumstances determines the nature of their personal reality, cognitively and emotionally. They are at the mercy of external occurrences, they are victims of the world, since the world is for them not a mere presence they can enjoy or contemplate, but is actually a box of tools that can prove itself to be useful or not, that can either function or not function, an attitude which makes them quite dependent on this world and its fluctuations. They lack the freedom of inner life, the ontological dimension that could provide them with freedom and tranquility. They instrumentalize the world, they instrumentalize themselves, they instrumentalize the relation to others, a source of much insecurity, unhappiness and pain. One important problem that this creates is that reality is not perceived in itself but only through the prism of some determined needs, a life loaded with expectations. The mind is therefore not free to modify its interpretations, it does not accept the world as a gratuitous offering, it is not allowed as well to capture events and entities in their inner dimension. This distorted and fixed view condemns the subject to a passive and distressing outlook, where he is primarily at odds with the world. He is blinded by his feelings, his pleasure and pain, satisfaction and dissatisfaction, and of course he is always worrying about the future, this ceaseless source of uncertainty, where he can always project his fears and imagine the worst. The freedom or being that provides the work of introspection escapes him completely.

Circumstantial thinking, through the dependency it engenders, one being submitted to the chaos and arbitrariness of the world, is a source of irritation and anger. The subject is not centered on himself, he is alienated, he is exocentered, offbeat within himself, disharmonious, he permanently endures a feeling of self-discrepancy. Therefore, he might experience a need to refocus, to retire into himself, to enjoy his inner being, a shift which might occur through different types of practices, such as praying, physical exercise, contemplation, rigorous dieting, intellectual activities, artistic practice, meditation, or diverse types of ascetic ritual. One of the hidden or explicit purposes of those activities is to install internal peace, and it is achieved through withdrawal from the world back to oneself. It is supposed to decrease the reactivity to the outside, taking distance from the world, reduce external dependency, and somehow stabilize the internal state. One gets back to oneself, doesn't merely respond to the demands from the world and reduces or abandons his expectations from this external world, relying more on oneself, an operation that can indeed reveal itself quite successful and pleasant. Unfortunately, many individuals are refractory to this psychological or ontological necessity, it frightens them, they prefer to ignore it or even openly criticize it, claiming its uselessness.

But just like in the reverse process, the dependency on the external world, the focus on the internal world encounters the challenge of the reality principle: a fundamental ontological dualism, where everything engenders its contrary, all entities and processes necessarily bearing their own power of negativity. As Aristotle warned us: opposites are born together. Thus, just as outer dependency can provoke a discrepancy, so does internal dependency, since one cannot avoid the inner-outer dialectical relation, constitutive of reality. All entities have an inner reality, be they endowed with consciousness or not, while they cannot avoid facing the interrelations they have to other entities, to the world as a whole. Thus, if one can indeed find some inner peace when he folds upon his inner self, he can easily forget that he cannot confine himself there and reside there eternally, he will sooner or later have to face again the harsh and uncontrollable outer reality. Although such a subject probably has encountered as well that his inner reality is not as docile and pleasant as he would wish it to be. But still, he more had the impression of being "at home" and relaxed, when being plunged in the world afflicts us in a stronger way with a feeling of estrangement, a scattered otherness being rather disturbing for our mental peace. Thus the subject might discover that his intimate self as well has a circumstantial dimension, since various inner obstacles condition our mental state, confining our tranquility and sense of freedom to a particular context, to a particular modality of being.

When plunged into oneself, one gets an impression of immediate connection with the "universe", with the totality, even with the absolute, since the "I" becomes the ultimate and exclusive reality. Often, in such practices of "diving in oneself", there is no real analysis, no substantial thinking, we are merely undergoing an experience, what can be called pre-reflective consciousness. Activities with some spiritual or intellectual pretensions can lack a critical dimension, the "outer" perspective than could show the inatity, vanity, uselessness, powerlessness, limitation or absurdity of such an exercise of introspection or withdrawal. This critical dimension will appear only when we will inevitably have to face the world again, a world that will impose on us its own reality, radically other than ours. But in this "inner voyage", we can lose our capacity for availability, since we have the impression of being in control of reality, we finally are in the "right place". We therefore do not welcome this world, that seems to us aggressive, unpleasant, terribly foreign to our own self. Basically, we would be in peace if there was no "outside". Although one might criticize the illusory dimension of such a statement, since very often, if we look at it properly, the outside terribly and "magically" resembles our inside. Already, because in both described cases we do not convey an ontological view of the world, since both schemes are conditional and circumstantial. This is the case for two reasons. The first one is an instrumentalization of the world and our self, since things and beings are there to provide us with pleasure and satisfy us rather than be taken in themselves. The second one is our refusal of finiteness, we are spurred by an excessive desire of immediacy, of totality, of absolute, which leads us to reject the "poverty" of reality. In both cases, we are therefore not available to being, everything becomes circumstantial. In our mind, everything is circumstantial because nothing is endowed with a true legitimacy, everything is fundamentally "in the way", everything is ultimately an obstacle. If the subject is ready to grant some justification to the rare events or situations that seem to conforme his desires and expectations, he can only accept what confirms his world vision. Unconsciously, we are competing with some omnipotent God who has to be satisfied.

While we are discussing this matter, we have in mind a very popular actual trend towards eastern influenced practices such as meditation and yoga, promoted as the panacea for existential or psychological problems, viewed as a form of enlightenment. And we have noticed a pattern among those practitioners, at least those we have met: a certain anti-intellectual posture, and a rather sensitive attitude, easily irritable, that seems to contradict the nature and purpose of their "spiritual" activity. One explanation is given by the famous or controversial guru Osho, a strong advocate of meditation, who at the same time criticizes it as a mere therapy. This would imply on one side that the people who find a need to get involved in such practices already encounter certain personal difficulties they cannot deal with otherwise, and at the same time the practice functions as a palliative, merely to alleviate the pain, but not deal more profoundly with existential problems. We could compare such an endeavor to any religious practices or rituals, the way they are commonly shared, that have an appeasing function by relating to some form or other of absolute, but do not provide a real challenge to the individual, in the sense that it remains very often superficial. Whether under the guise of science or spirituality, a naive, uncritical, or at least non-critical attitude is established, usually based on an established theory or doctrine. One striking feature of the phenomenon is the idea of being "beyond the mental", which has the usefulness of proposing an activity that interrupts the constant uncontrolled worrying that afflicts numerous individual, but at the same time it throws the baby with the bathwater by criticizing and avoiding a real and substantial thinking practice. They confuse worrying and thinking, a common prejudice. Thus, when those people emerge from their momentary nirvana, maybe they have somewhat calmed down, a useful recourse, but they have not worked at all the adequate cognitive competencies necessary to deal with the world. If those persons already have such thinking practice, it might not represent a problem, but if they don't, which seems the case to us for a vast majority, they feel powerless, they go back to their anxiety and their anger about a world that does not fit their expectations, where they feel misunderstanding and being misunderstood. They fall in the trap of what we call circumstantial thinking, since the chaos and unpredictability of the world come as an impediment to the internal peace they so much desire, they easily feel victimized. So when one is confronted with the necessity to think or to analyze, it gives an impression of fracture within the longed-for unity, a disappointment which causes irritation. One momentarily managed to have a pleasant unified connection and now one has to reluctantly go step by step through a laborious process of thought examination, imposed by the reality of the world.

Quite often, even though some gurus warn against this drawback viewed as a weakness, there is a clear cut opposition between the adepts' attitude during meditation and their posture in daily life. The accepting and contemplating attitude they work on when they are alone with themselves or their little group does not apply once they emerge from their isolation and return to their existential routine. Funnily enough, instead of calming down the anger or anxiety of the subject, this schizophrenic behavior can on the contrary produce or intensify negative and destructive emotions, because of the frustration. Hence, such practices tend to reinforce a narcissistic and egocentric behavior, an unhappy narcissism, exactly the contrary of what it is supposed to accomplish. Thus we view this practice as a form of circumstantial thinking, since it is conditioned by a specific context, it depends on it, it lacks the freedom of ontological thinking, free and unconditioned. Such a conditional tranquility, we call it comfort, since it is momentarily determined in space and time, and it comes in opposition with "real" tranquility, which is unconditional since it only depends on the freedom and determination of the individual and not on some situation or mental paraphernalia. The real test for such practices is to examine if for the subject the world is a gift or rather a threat, a challenge or rather a misfortune, if not an abomination.

In this context, we should mention what we can call an economy of narcissism, which does not last long and remains relatively superficial. We identify with characters, real or fictional –television series have a lot to do with it –, we prefer such an individual or such a group, we love one and we hate the other, until we get tired and find other affinities. We follow this or that specialist or influencer, we belong to a given fan club. Infatuation and depression follow one another, fantasies and a return to a reality that imposes itself, outer jail alternate with inner jail.

It can be difficult to be honest, authentic, and true. This requires accepting oneself, despites the ugly and the bad, but also being ready to deploy this imperfection in the world. Ontological thinking makes the ugly and the bad visible, as it penetrates to the root of the subject or the object it examines. Circumstantial thinking, on the contrary, offers a nice trick to make reality a bit more acceptable, to improve its appearance, to make it at least less horrible. For example, if the traffic is bad, it is annoying when we are in it, but it makes the delay acceptable, it could almost enter some sort of divine plan. It is no one's fault. However, if someone would say, "I am late because I didn't want to come", or "I am late because I partied last night and didn't wake up this morning", he can be criticized or even suffer retaliation. More authenticity implies more "ugliness". This doesn't look like God's plan, this looks more like a capricious or an irresponsible choice.

The French nineteenth century writer Stendhal invites us to locate in an era the crystallization of certain values. Such an exercise would allow us to identify the circumstantial dimension of what could seem to be a freely determined thought. Thus, in our time, we notice an aestheticization or a cosmeticization of existence, a promotion of pleasure, health and well-being, rather than wasting time in sacrificing oneself in earning a living or being useful. This can designate another form of rationality, another type of common sense. We are festive, playful, dreamlike, imaginative and creative, as if the repression of previous generations were coming back in force: then we had to be reasonable. The holistic scheme prevails, as a kind of spiritual materialism. We entertain a new relationship to technology, quite contradictory. Both a suspicion of massive, large-scale technologies and of science, considered unnatural and dangerous, and a passion for those microtechnologies that modify our personal daily lives, a source of comfort on which we become extremely dependent. We appreciate the cozy repose of "cocooning", when in good company we watch endless television series. The vital, vigorous and combative drive is no longer appropriate. Relatively passive, we oscillate between boredom and irritation, because things do not go as we would like and we are sensitive, a certain existential flatness punctuated by minor enthusiasms. Our ideals remain quite domestic, but we are charitable, we have compassion, and evil frightens us without fighting it. We feel overwhelmed and threatened by a world order that does not suit us. But our ideal remains rather anemic, because social engagement is hardly appropriate or motivating. We protest from home, discreetly, by expressing ourselves on social networks, by giving to charity. Great schemes such as progress or far-reaching political projects fade away or are criticized: we are left in politics with the vague unanimous – sometimes illusory – idea of "liberal democracy". Although we are mainly talking about Western culture here, because contrary to certain forecasts which had imposed themselves, we are witnessing the emergence of a strong multipolar world, where many differences and tensions are expressed, sometimes violently, between cultures and traditions.

Feelings, admiration, horror, pity or sympathy, replace action. The established and official authorities are somewhat undermined. The power is either hidden, through opaque industrial and financial structures, lobbies and social manipulations, or it comes "from below", from the masses, through social networks and its various movements. We can see in such a device of freedom and diverse technologies the possibility for each one to express himself as he wants and to find his moments of personal glory in order to be seen and heard as he likes. He can be keen on selling his own image, a motivating endeavor. We can thus share our passions, our problems, our dreams and our pains. One can belong to such or such tribe which is not geographically determined, since one is not bound to his family or original place. Social bonds are governed by elective affinities. Fashions and fads are engendered hastily in this mobile matrix, or disappear just as quickly, information, true or false, spread there without concern for real censorship, especially when they arouse passions; they are modified with always the same candor and an equal sincerity. Minorities, however diverse they may be, can form communities without difficulty. Reason is no longer required, the rule is the absence of a determined center, the reign is that of multiplicity and diversity. Multiple myths and spiritualities abound, which despite their apparent diversity share the same interpretative paradigms, the same prejudices predominate. For example, the criticism of utilitarianism, the apology of presentism, the cult of the natural, with of course strong resistance here and there, depending on the place and the individual, debate must go on.

Chapter 2

Ontological thinking

Ontology, as a branch of philosophy, is the domain of examining the nature of being and existence. Literally, it is the "knowledge of being". It tries to characterize and categorize the different types of "objects" we can encounter, examine their structures and their relations. In simple terms, ontology seeks the classification and explanation of entities, abstract or concrete, material or spiritual. Ontological thinking means to go beyond the immediate context, behind mere appearances, circumstances, activities and details of phenomena, using analytic reason in order to examine reality and its constitution, in order to understand the nature and causality of its elements. It looks for the "essence" of the objects, in opposition to the "accidents" they can undergo, it attempts to capture the eternity of an entity rather than its contingency, its nature rather than its diverse predicates: appearance, variable features, actions, utility, etc. Unless these very features are actually essential to the definition of the entity. For example, we can define a "rock" without any preoccupation with its shape or utility, but defining a "fork" implies to account for its structure and its purpose, which are both fundamentally constitutive of the object.

Here, we must establish a specificity for the general category of object called "subject". We can speak of "subject" for any object, since such a concept is defined as the central substance or core of an entity as opposed to its attributes, as we already indicated it. But what we wish to address now is a more restrictive definition of a subject. In this case the subject is not only the immediate cause of an action, like any other subject can be, as in the "rock broke the window", but can deliberately decide upon an action. Not just as an animal, guided primarily by its instinct and its sensitivity, but endowed with a thinking and conscious mind, capable of willful deliberation and decision. It therefore has an "ego", an "I", which he can distinguish from the external reality. This capacity of free will will entail that we can pass judgments on his actions and behavior, basing ourselves on various modalities of reason, such as practical considerations, morality, values, etc. In this sense, we can distinguish two aspects of his being: his general nature, characteristics and constitution, what can be called his internal necessity, and his freedom, the way he decides upon his own behavior. In a broad way, we can therefore distinguish an ontological explanation when we account for his internal features, and a circumstantial explanation when we account for external factors. But a new problem arises, since we can observe an actual fracture between an a priori essence of this subject and the existence of a free will that does not necessarily coincide and can often oppose each other. For example, the desire to survive, inherent to all living beings, and the opposite capacity for self-abnegation or self-sacrifice, which depends on the will of the individual. This opposition will lead for existential philosophers to the idea that for the human individual "Existence precedes essence", which implies that we all have a distinct essence, determined by the thoughts, experiences, decisions and actions that compose the narrative of our personal life. This occurs in opposition to a rather naturalist or essentialist perspective where human essence is defined a priori, therefore defining us as a general category rather than an individual entity. An ontological thinking tends to identify the nature and inclination of entities, its modality of decision making, rather than to explain events through a general specific finality. Thus, this "nature" can never be invoked as a reason in itself, since there must be a dimension of freewill in the assessment of the subject.

Nevertheless, the context cannot be totally ignored. There is a dialectical relationship between an efficient cause, a mechanical or material explanation, and a final cause, an essential or spiritual explanation, both analysis which can either be in phase or in contradiction. An ontological analysis remains conscious of the modality of the speech, since no speech is without any modality, it is always grounded in some paradigm, loaded with presuppositions. A statement cannot pretend to some pure factuality or pure objectivity, even when it thinks it is considering the totality of things or grasping some quintessence. On the reverse, the circumstantial thinker generally lacks distance from himself, remains unconscious of himself, stuck in a dogmatic scheme of certitude and strong belief. The former is rather authentic, capable of critical thinking, while the latter is sincere, he believes in his feelings.

Let us now attempt to specify our personal understanding of an ontological account, an ontological type of thinking, in opposition to a circumstantial one when it comes to understanding a human being, his behavior and his actions. In response to our previous explanations, one could claim that to base ourselves on an a priori human nature or essence to explain the actions and behavior of an individual is ontological, since such an account is based on the internal identity and constitution of this entity and not purely on external factors. Formally, we could say that this objection is in a way relevant, since we speak about what we are and we somewhat grant ourselves in this fashion the status of an autonomous subject, a human being, and not merely of an object, as would be an entity entirely moved by outside forces. Here, as we already explained, different philosophical postures, worldviews or paradigms might oppose each other on this matter. So let us explain why ultimately, after some hesitation, we decided to classify essentialist types of explanation, such as "our nature or our character is the cause of our actions", as a circumstantial one. The primary reason is that we consider that "being"is not a mere intellectual or formal concept, but it derives from an experience: "being"is an encounter with our self, as an individual, we live it in the soul and the flesh, and through this confrontation we engage in universality, we struggle with reality, the world and ourselves, through this encounter we articulate our free will and our existence. Thus Sartre opposes the "being in-itself", endowed with a fixed essence and a specific function, plunged in a predefined world, and the "being for-itself", endowed with a conscience and a free existence, thrown into a mobile and undetermined world. We are not determined by some essence. We must indeed recognize there are some strong "natural inclinations"in ourselves, and we have to acknowledge the presence of necessity, but we must grant a crucial function to free will, if only the permanent, very human choice to live or die. The essence determines the object, not the human, for the capacity of alienation is a fundamental human characteristic. In order words, our decisions make us who we are, and not the reverse, where some essence would determine our decisions, as is the case for animals, through instinct.

In this sense, as Heidegger and others grappled with, we have to distinguish "being"and "Being". The term "being"refers to some particular determination, the identity of some entity that distinguishes itself from others in a given way because of an apriori nature, which makes it the element of a specific category, putting together those sharing the same characteristics. While "Being" is what allows things "to be", it is the emergence, the surging of a radical singularity. The term "being" indicates the "what is": things and thoughts, objects and subjects, properties and relations, while "Being" indicates "the 'is' of what is", that which makes them present as beings, and present as the beings that they are, a rather transcendent determination. In a different framework, more Christian, Nicolas Cusanus distinguishes both conceptions of being as "other" and "not-other", the former referring to finiteness, the second to the infinite and the absolute, what belongs to the divine. For indeed, what is "not-other" is itself undefinable, plastic and thus free, since in general we define any fixed entity through the fact that it is other than any other, through what formally distinguishes it from other entities. What is "not-other", thereby escaping the principle of identity and any categorization, remains radically singular.

Ontology is literally, etymologically, a "knowledge of being", or as we think, an "experience of being". And the substance, the root of such an encounter is our face to face with "Being", in a transcendent sense, the principle, entity or non-entity that accounts from beings to be and be what they are, or the "not-being" which allows beings to be. In this sense, "Being" is characterized by some radical freedom. Or by an absolute subjectivity, the subjectivity or the "over-subjectivity", the subjectivity of a "non-subject", since its transcending subjectivity is indistinguishable from the subjectivity of any other subject, for any comparison would be incommensurable and absurd. In a way, "Being" cannot be distinguished from different "beings", or between different "beings", just like "Unity" cannot be distinguished from different numbers or between different numbers, since all numbers equally possess this unity, since all numbers are a particular form of unity. Just like God cannot be really distinguished from created beings, since all created beings are nothing else than the manifestation of the creating power. In a different cultural matrix, the Chinese daoist philosopher Zhuangzi would say that the only true identity of any human being is unique: it is the "Dao", the principle of all principles, the "what makes things what they are", the "what makes things do what they do". The Dao is the first necessity, the grounding of all necessity, the radical "non-place" or "non-entity" that cannot be spoken, the grounding of any true freedom.

Nevertheless, the difficulty of distinguishing circumstantial and ontological understanding of an individual is encountered in the Bible, when it is said that God only can truly judge a man, "his heart and loins", what can be called his subjectivity, what "moves" him, instead of the human, limited, which perceives only the outside, the fixed and the formal, the appearance. And it is specified that "he that searches the hearts knows what is the mind of the Spirit", in other words, when we perceive adequately this singular subjectivity, which always redefines itself, we have access to the transcendent. Therefore, as soon as we confine our own being to some fixed and distinct nature, essence or entity, we enter the domain of circumstances, we estrange ourselves from the experience of Being. First, because we lose the perspective of radical freedom that characterizes "Being". Second, because we objectify ourselves, we lose our status as subjects, since we are not the actual autonomous cause of our own behavior and actions. Third, through this fixed nature or essence, we alienate ourselves, we dissent from our own groundless grounding, we become the passive and powerless victim or object of a predetermined fate. Fourth, we lose touch with any attempt to access Being, in spite of the fragility and limit of any such attempts.

Being can be approached in different ways: as the unconditional, the first cause, the self-cause, the radical transcendence, the self-negation, the unthinkable or unspeakable from which all thoughts or speech emerge, the unprincipled principle that allows any speech or thought, any creation. Therefore, explaining our behavior and actions through some established and fixed nature or essence can be considered circumstantial and not ontological, since we confuse the contingent or arbitrary with the essential and free, just like when we attribute the cause of our actions or behavior to some external factors. In fact, with the concepts of an established "personal nature" or "individual essence", we are actually externalizing ourselves, we are giving up on our true self which is a non-self, we are abandoning the dimension of substantial freedom constitutive of our being.

Therefore, in order to capture the reality of a subject, and to determine the substantial cause for his deeds, one should be invited to think deeper than external facts and the general situation. This implies to think about the person itself, directly, instead of focusing on the context and the immediate external cause, instead of viewing the subject as a reactive entity deprived of any free will. Ontological thinking invites us to focus upon one's scheme, its functioning, its worldview, its specific goals and desires. But for this, we must deconstruct the subject's speech, the myth he fabricated, analyze his attitude, identify his individual nature, and not remain in the domain of what does not fundamentally and specifically intrinsically belong to him. Of course, our point is not to exclude from the explanation the circumstantial character of a situation, which can of course be a part of the reality, but rather to show the limits and the problems of those circumstances and how they affect the thinking and the essence of the being without really determining his actions and behavior.

The psychological tendencies, nature or identity of a subject can belong to both circumstantial and ontological thinking, a difference which is sometimes hard to establish, since the fine line separating them can be quite blurry. But we can still propose some ways of distinguishing their utilization. The main difference is how we relate to this "identification". If it is a new discovery, or if it represents a challenge, then we can qualify its usage as ontological. This new discovery can as well be a rediscovery, since we can permanently discover our own self. Astonishment is probably the most important emotion in philosophy, a sign of availability. If one is available, he will notice what he had not noticed before, or what he had forgotten, or even denied. Thus he will notice "again" and "again" who he is, a sort of permanent discovery. If the mind is alive, it does not allow itself the complacency of hackneyed circumstantial arguments. If our "way of being" is an argument we use in order to explain our behavior in a lazy manner, where we feel self-justified since "things are like this", then we can view this as a circumstantial explanation, since it is presented as an immutable order of the world, as an unchangeable internal context. We could here distinguish "apparent ontological" speech, which tries to justify, and "genuine ontological" speech, which tries to explain. The main goal of an explanation is to make a phenomenon understandable, clarifying its process by giving the most appropriate and significant reasons for its occurrence. The main goal of a justification is to provide a "good" reason why something exists, a speech is said or an act committed, protecting the subject from any accusation or incrimination, or by reducing his culpability, attenuating the weight of his guilt. Both verbs, to explain and to justify, are often confused, it can be difficult to distinguish them, and indeed resorting to the principle of justification might sometimes be more appropriate, although it is excessively and unconsciously practiced, but we should remember what fundamentally distinguishes them.

For ontological thinking, two main criteria are involved: freedom and consciousness. The latter implies self-consciousness, for consciousness without self-consciousness would be a rather mechanical operation. Freedom implies a deliberate choice, "I am like this because I want to be like this". But it can as well take another form, more grounded in necessity: "I am like this, I admit it, I fully choose it and accept to be so", or "I am like this but I refuse it, I am fighting against it". In both cases we take full responsibility for this "nature", even if it is imposed on us, either because I make this situation "mine", fully adopting my own inclinations, or because I have not been able yet to modify it but I actively wish to do so and I am on it. For consciousness, if it is an "adequate" consciousness, I am not only conscious of this psychological and existential reality, a consciousness of the world and myself, but I am conscious as well of the diverse problems it entails, in which case I remain available to any possibility of modification, even when it sounds a priori rather impossible. Consciousness is therefore viewed as a challenge, not as a fatality. This implies that the concept of "nature", including "my nature", will not be used and abused to explain any problem, since as much as possible we will leave room for some deliberate self-determination. For example, the fact I am an "angry person" is not sufficient to explain every fit of anger I have, since there is still some possibility of avoiding angry reactions in any specific situations. Therefore self-consciousness implies a more refined and problematic understanding of the nature of this anger, of its implications and consequences. It remains a challenge, because there are still some moments where I could have avoided giving in to this anger, by observing its mechanisms and genesis, and through learning to control myself. The "nature" of this self-consciousness should not exclude any self-challenge, or it would be bad faith.

One way to identify circumstantial thinking and distinguish it from ontological thinking can be observed within the dynamic of dialogue, particularly in rational dialogue of the socratic type, but as well in usual discussions. We can notice it by the discrepancies between the questions and the answers, by the lack of coherence which often indicates an escape or an attempt at self-justification. For example through the shift taking place between the "general"and the "particular", a phenomenon that is often not clearly identified but intuitively perceived. Let us give an example: "Why did you lie? Because everybody lies". "Are you a liar? I had no choice at that moment, in order to avoid a conflict". The first stratagem uses "human nature"as a way to avoid accounting for the singular lie, replacing the personal issue by a general one. The second stratagem uses a particular context to avoid dealing with a more general problem about one's personality. In both cases we can notice that any dimension of freedom is denied, by providing some grounding to a "I had to", which is to say "It was not possible otherwise". From this observation, we can conclude that both general and particular can be used as a circumstantial justification, be it the "nature of things"or a "particular constraint". This can make us conclude that an important difference between an ontological explanation and a circumstantial one is the authenticity of the answer, the fact we take on the challenge that is brought to us. It is not merely a formal problem, purely logical as some critics might voice, but one of attitude. For even if most people are not so attentive to logical issues in a conscious way, it seems to us that we are endowed with a preconscious rationality, what can be called common sense, that guides our thoughts and speech. Therefore, any obvious breach in the rational process necessarily indicates an attempt to avoid and self-justify, an obvious problem of the circumstantial rationale. Being is of the order of reason, in the sense that reality is composed of links such as, causality, conditions, implications, consequences and other constitutive interconnections, and we have to grasp them in order to claim any understanding. Of course, reason does not exhaust our grasp of reality, since numerous phenomena are beyond our understanding, and our subjectivity plays a crucial role, but as much as possible, reason is the means by which we reach consciousness. Although we should here distinguish a reduced form of rationality and reason in a broader sense, which implies for example emotions and creativity. Therefore any ontological thinking needs a rational dimension, without which it simply tries to avoid the reality principle.

A specific aspect of the difference between the two types of thinking is well illustrated but the blatant asymmetry that characterizes the way we describe other people's mistakes and shortcomings, in particular those we don't appreciate, and our own, or the ones of people we like. The negative aspect of the "enemies" takes an ontological or essentialist turn: that is the way they are, that is their nature or their deep self. As for "our people" and ourselves, those same defects are described as unfortunate, unlucky, accidental, they are primarily due to some inopportune circumstances, an unfavorable conjuncture, or some adverse external cause. For example: "He is like that" versus "I was forced" or "He reaps what he has sown" versus "I could not avoid this situation"... In a war, the enemy is fundamentally bad, when "we" are just trying to protect ourselves or to defend our vital interests. Such an unfair discrepancy shows how much we instinctively perceive, understand and master, at least in a pre-reflexive mode, the difference between the ontological and the circumstantial way of thinking. In this context, we should bring up as well the "deep down" argument, used again to protect the "good people", "our people", from any criticism. Its dynamic is to impute any problem to a type of exteriority, inconsequential, since "deep down", in his true inner self, this person is a good person. Thus, for example, the worst criminal is fundamentally "good" because he takes "good" care of his family. His crimes have therefore a mere superficial, accidental, unsubstantial nature, circumstantial, they should not really count in the assessment of the individual, essentially good. "My son is a good boy, I know him, I am his mother", is a great classic. A real contradiction, since "being his mother"is rather the opposite of "knowing him" : nothing is more blind than the love of a mother. But in these various types of argument, we can see how an "essential" is used in a circumstantial way, since it ignores all freedom, all accounts of reality.

In this context, we should mention an instance that we call "false ontological speech". It generally takes the form of "wise sentences", such as "That's life", "That's the way things are", "Everything comes and goes", etc. They are often used to counter some dramatic speech or behavior, and as such they can act as an actual ontological speech, since they make the interlocutor conscious of his attitude, confronting him about his excessively tragic behavior and obsession with particular circumstances. But the tricky dimension of such expressions can be identified when the locutor uses those sentences in order to justify himself, or to justify his impotence and grant himself a sense of "good conscience". As well, instead of proposing some healthy distance, it can rather be the demonstration of a lack of empathy, even a cruel indifférence, and the fine line between both stances can be rather difficult to perceive. The claim that "everything is normal"can represent either an expression of passive fatalism or an attempt to free oneself from the "extraordinary"and emotional dimension of the circumstances, it can be an expression of bad faith or the manifestation of self-challenge. Thus we have to examine to what extent it appropriately fits the situation, if it invites the subject to think or to stop thinking, as a mere tool of self-protection, if one remains available to the situation or closes himself up.

Let us now examine the issue of time. Time is a major aspect of reality, determined by the sequence of events, by their chronology, with which we must interact. We must adapt to it, but we must as well freely "construct" our own time, by determining for example priorities, or choosing our time frame or rhythm. Circumstances are inscribed in time, be they external circumstances or internal ones, and our freedom is articulated in the way we relate to those circumstances. The circumstantial thinking defines itself blindly through some objectively defined time frame, be it internal or external obligations, deprived of any interplay with a personal freewill. It negates the existential dimension of time, for example with psychological needs or external necessities, there is no room for a transcending subject and his power over time, there is no "playing" with time. In this sense there is a problematic externalization of the self, even in relation to internal issues, since the subject is in a real sense alienated from itself through these so-called needs. Prisoner of our internal time, we are like an infant deprived of any self-control. Prisonner of external time, we are like a slave who is always told what to do. At the same time, we must be conscious of those temporal circumstances, otherwise they will catch up on us and impose their harsh reality. Ignoring circumstantial reality engenders a diktat of new circumstances: we end up paying the price. Like for the person who tries to ignore the traffic, the person who tries to ignore his internal clock, be it biological or psychological, will necessarily suffer some retribution. But the blind and passive trailing of circumstances as well will engender some form of penalty.

In a paradoxical way, we have to acknowledge that the person prisoner of his internal time will tend to be a prisoner of external time as well, and vice versa. Maybe not initially or superficially, since both dimensions are formally opposed, but in the long run, because such individuals have developed a given attitude: a lack of plasticity, a lack of distance, a lack of potency, a lack of freedom. What can be considered a form of immaturity, a certain difficulty to manage reality and relate to it. They are caught in the "great chain of needs", no matter the origin or nature of those needs. And of course this always brings them some opportune justification, since they can hence answer any criticism with "I had a need". But this need is considered as an implacable obligation, rather than as a challenge for the freedom of being.

In order to conclude our exposition of the distinction between circumstantial thinking and ontological thinking, let us take up again the example of the person who is late. The first type of circumstantial argument is the external circumstances: "There was a lot of traffic", "My wife held me up", etc. It will rather focus on a context, on external reasons, on other persons, on the state of the world. The second type of circumstantial argument is the internal circumstances: "I am careless about time", "I was distracted", etc., when this type of argument is recurrent, when it is used as a complacent leitmotif or as a justification. This type of apparent ontological thinking tries to focus on the general scheme of the subject, his functioning, his vision of the world, his difficulty with reality, his fear of the world, his lack of commitment, etc., exposed as some immutable feature of his self. Such elements will be more revealing about the person than external circumstances, it might allow us to understand the individual better, but alas it is rather used as a circumstance, as some "essential"and frozen feature of reality. The argument is rather ontological when the person admits his deliberate choice: "I decided to take my time", or "I chose to take the risk of a fluid traffic", and from these statements he can concretely "discover"his carelessness, his thoughtlessness, his irresponsibility. Nevertheless, he admits that he made a choice, with the implications of such a choice. But it is often difficult to identify and to admit our deliberate decisions in our daily routines, we tend to favor the principles of "habits"or "fortuitousness"as a way to escape the responsibility for our actions.

Chapter 3

Circumstantial thinking (CT) and ontological thinking (OT)

Let us now examine in a different way what are the fundamental differences between the modality of circumstantial thinking and the ontological modality of thinking. We will oppose the CT: circumstantial thinker to the OT: ontological thinker through different conceptual oppositions. We will use as a recurrent example the law of gravitation. It should be noted that all human beings operate in parallel on these two levels, circumstantial and ontological, in varying proportions. But much of this is done unconsciously, especially the first one, which can be described as more "natural". Because it is necessary to carry out work on oneself to pass to a more ontological level, since it implies an increased self-awareness.

Complaint/Joy The CT complains that things are not the way he wants, he does not appreciate reality, which for him is accidental and undesirable, he suffers from it. The OT enjoys reality, he accepts it as it is, for him events are constitutive of this reality and it would be ridiculous to complain about this reality. We can here mention the "amor fati" of Nietzsche, the ineluctability of fate as an object of desire and joy. Thus the CT complains that things are unstable, heavy, and fall, while the OT joyfully lives in a world where gravitation is the rule, with the diverse possibilities it offers.

Endure/Play   The CT passively undergoes unfortunate events, the sad nature of reality, contrary to his expectations. The OT understands the underlying rules of the game and he plays with it. The CT undergoes gravitation, he endures its heaviness and imposition. The OT plays with gravitation, by throwing balls, jumping or launching rockets, viewing gravitation as a challenge and not a burden.

Immediacy/Consciousness   The CT views each event as some singular, accidental and unpredictable event, a perception amplified by the unwanted and unpleasant nature of the phenomena. This can be called a reductionist worldview. The OT views each singular event as an integral part of a wider reality of which he is conscious. He entertains a broader and deeper worldview, where the immediate is only a reflection of a more fundamental reality, the emergence of underlying processes. The CT periodically observes falling objects and he fears their fall. The OT permanently observes the power of gravitation in his various interactions with opposite forces.

Pragmatic/Esthetic   The CT entertains diverse agendas, wishing and fearing diverse phenomena, he privileges practical specific initiatives. It is a needy form of thinking. The OT contemplates the actions and forms of reality and events, he privileges attentive scrutiny and meditation, pondering over the nature of the world as a whole, as an infinite aggregate of parts. He promotes an attitude of acceptance instead of a needy attitude. The CT is concerned with multiple specific objects and structures. The OT contemplates the harmony of the world and its interaction with specific entities, he focuses on some important projects, unconcerned with ancillary details.

Although we can also problematize the term "pragmatic". Often we mean by "pragmatic" or "practical" what is most immediately applicable, we mean merely by these terms what is the easiest, what is the most obvious or empirical, avoiding a more substantial usage or meaning of the concept. Therefore, ideas or thinking are in themselves considered impractical, since their aim is unworldly and more ethereal, although more crucial and necessary. But if practicality refers to a capacity for prompt effort and energy over doubt or delay, challenge and self-accomplishment instead of measly material tasks, intellectual activity can be considered indeed quite practical.

Accidental/Necessary   The CT views events as accidents, lucky or unlucky, desirable or undesirable, the OT perceives events as a coherent manifestation of necessity, including in its fortuitous dimension. When an object falls, the CT views it as an accident, or as the product of a specific efficient cause considered negative. The OT views this falling object as a manifestation of a coherent law of nature, he actually sees the principle of gravitation, and not just mere objects.

Heteronomous/Self-sufficient   The CT depends a lot on external events to determine his own mental state, he is therefore anxious, unstable and regretful. He strongly depends on the judgment of others, from which the need to justify himself. The OT is equanimous, he willfully determines his mental state, independently of external events, remaining distant as well from his own emotional reactions. The CT's satisfaction depends on the falling or stability of objects. The OT's satisfaction depends on his unity with the fundamental nature of things, he is therefore not affected or lightly so by the diversity of "falling" events.

Impulsion/Freedom   The CT expresses his freedom through his momentary relation to specific phenomena, that he wants or does not want, whimsically changing his mind according to circumstances, external or internal modifications. He wants things to fall or not to fall, hopeful and anxious that events will satisfy his desires, witnessing his freedom only when occurrences correspond to his expectations. The OT articulates his freedom in relation to his understanding of necessity and general processes, with which he interacts, which makes his expression of freedom relatively constant. He expresses this freedom through distance and detachment from particular events or puny satisfactions. This does not stop him from desiring specific happenings, but he maintains a higher or transcendent perspective on his expectations and actions, problematizing his own worries and desires.

Dramatic/Peaceful   The CT nurtures a dramatic relation to the world and to events. Numerous banal phenomena are easily taken as some extraordinary occurrence, sad or joyful. He easily falls into hyperbolic speech and intense emotions, he can be easily rather tragic or indignant. The CT tends to suffer from chronic insatisfaction, since he is very focused on the circumstances, expecting a lot from them, a greed that can never be quite satisfied.

The OT maintains a rather peaceful relation to reality, where there is little room for the extraordinary, although he can permanently be astonished by the banal and the ordinary. The CT is surprised by unexpected falling objects, which in general is an unpleasant exception, contrary to his expectations. The OT is rather surprised by the non-falling objects, even though it is the majority of cases, since he has little expectations and reality is for him a permanent source of amazement and wonder.

Partial/Dialectical The CT permanently takes sides, he divides the world in parts, he chooses, he frequently opts for or against something, criticizing, ignoring or refusing the opposite side. He easily defines what is positive and what is negative, often in a rigid and passionate way. From this standpoint, common sense or reason is easily perceived as an intrusion, as an alienation, as a breach in the protection of his integrity. The OT recognizes that opposites are born together, that they feed each other, that they attract each other. He recognizes the illusory dimension of taking sides, although this does not stop him from taking options, but he remains conscious of the consequences, implications and limits of such a choice. He maintains an overview of opposite tensions, instead of falling in the manic depressive system of winning and losing, of satisfaction and dissatisfaction. He is aware that positive and negative are often reversible values, depending on a given context, within different scales, reduced or enlarged, or within different time frames. For example, according to the principle of enantiodromia, any value turns into its opposite through a natural tendency to excess. Thus, the person who does not like gravitation because it makes things heavier to transport does not realize that gravitation as well allows constructions to be stable.

Positivism/Hermeneutics The CT tends to be an empiricist, he sees the external world and facts as a direct source of knowledge, he takes his perceptions at face value, they constitute the meaning and content of truth. The OT grounds his thinking in reason, he sees the external world as a mediating point towards the meaning or discovery of truth, he needs interpretation. As a consequence, insofar as he belongs to the world, the CT perceives himself as an evidence, a clear and knowable object, while the OT perceives himself as a mere possibility, a subject of his own thinking in his infinite search for the meaning of truth. Therefore the fall of an object is for the CT perceived as an evidence, as an event in itself, when the OT tries to establish different types of interpretation of such a phenomenon, for example its existential implications or consequences, its practical or symbolic significance.

Morality/Reason   The CT is profoundly anchored in a system of "good and bad": there is what is good and what is bad, who is good and who is bad, what can be called a moral or ethical worldview. Things are divided between what is allowed and what is forbidden, it is a rigid system. He undergoes an ingrained sense of guilt, for oneself or others, which implies alternatively justification and punishment. For example, we ask "who started the fight", rather than knowing "why there is a fight". Circumstantial explanations are often used to attenuate the "badness" of a wrong action or to disculpate the suspected party, the justification. But fundamentally, everyone is guilty, otherwise there would be no need for justification. Thus the moral dimension, which incites the subject to justify himself, easily falls into circumstantial explanations, in order to aggravate or to extenuate the judgment. Ironically, the attempt to aggravate the blame, primarily directed towards others and not oneself, tends to enlarge the explanation through a higher level of causality or reality, by proving the fundamental evil of an individual beyond mere circumstances, thus provoking indignation. For ourselves, we prefer to believe in our good intentions, in the merits of our person beyond any particular circumstances. The OT rather attempts to use a broader sense of reason in order to identify fundamental processes and their power of determination. He as well can choose between good and bad, but he remains conscious of the relative dimension of his judgment. He stays available, generally avoiding indignation and other forms of emotional excess. But in general, nothing is a priori refused or prohibited, since everything has meaning, everything remains fluid: understanding is the priority. Good and bad are thus constantly problematized, since their evaluation depends largely on the width and depth of the analysis, varying with the chosen perspective. This does not imply that the OT rejects the idea of freedom and responsibility, but it means that one is accountable for his worldview and general attitude more than for a specific action, although the latter is not entirely denied, it is merely relativized.

In order to conclude, we can propose the distinction Nietzsche makes between three archetypes. The camel, who passively undergoes and suffers the weight of reality and its obligations. The lion, who angrily fights and rebels against reality and its constraints. The child, who contemplates reality and plays with it.

We could describe through different steps of causality the emergence of an ontological perspective out of a circumstantial one. First, In the most reduced level of causality, a given person or context is the cause of my action, the source of my problem or misery. I am determined by the outside, from the outside. Second, I realize that I am the cause of this problem, since I place myself in opposition to the otherness, I am reacting to it in an inappropriate manner, by allowing myself to be triggered by this externality. In this sense, this otherness reveals my own self or its tendencies, which I can try to modify by avoiding to react in a problematic way. Third, I realize I am the cause of such an externality, unconsciously or unwillingly. I provoke it, I attract it like a magnet attracting an opposite force. I realize that "I provide the stick to be beaten with", or "I made the rope with which to hang himself". And indeed many of our actions provoke unwanted reactions that we could complain about, until we realize that we were the cause of it. Some people manage to create a painful context around themselves, by which they feel afterwards victimized, when they did everything possible to engender such a context. In other words, my way of being is a primary cause of what is happening around me, I create my own world. Fourth, there is no causality, or there is a causality beyond causality, there is a mere coherence or symbiosis between me and the world. The otherness is not separate from me, we are interrelated, we mutually reflect each other, we cannot complain about the world since we are an integral part of it.

Thus, to summarize, the different steps are the following. I am passively affected by the outside. I am conscious of my reaction and I can react differently to outside. I am the cause of the outside. I am one with the outside, it is "my" coherent world. Let us examine the problem in a concrete way, through the person who arrives late because of traffic. First level: I am late because of traffic. Second level: I am late because I have a hard time managing my time, I could have left earlier to avoid traffic. Third level: I was affected by traffic because I am usually late, or I cause traffic problems because I take my car. Fourth: I live in a world of cars and traffic, of rushing and lateness.

The subject can consider himself an instrument of the world, a mere element of collective consciousness, progress, humanity, or any other universal reality, without thus annihilating and exhausting his own being, maintaining his irreplaceable singularity. Such a perspective can constitute a positive self-forgetfulness, meaningful and probably joyful. The problematic self-forgetfulness is the one that is spiteful. When we allow ourselves to be absorbed, to be gobbled up by the world, by others, or when we believe it is the case, and then we seek compensation, consolation or revenge for having thus been instrumentalized, since we feel we have been used as mere "fodder". In this case the abandonment of oneself to the world is purely instrumental and passive, recognition is sought. We were meek, we accepted our status of non-existence, we were compliant, we tried to please everyone, we sacrificed our being, we were not rewarded for our deeds, we gave up on ourselves, and there was no payback or gratitude. In a way, such a subject practices self-destruction, because of his own internal circumstances, not because of the outside ones.

In the second part of this work, we will try to analyze the different problems or features of the circumstantialization process, identifying the strategies for escaping the freedom of ontological thinking, and the implications for the subject himself.

Chapter 4

Externalization of the subject

"My car was broken"; "Traffic was difficult"; "My children needed me" … We hear those types of justification quite often, as explanations of different issues that can be identified and questioned. One thing they have in common, is that they all appear to give a ready-made explanation for events or actions, that usually will be sufficient for the interlocutor, for reasons of social conventions. Those arguments deal with the immediate, the practical, and visibly do not need further deepening. But, do they deal with the essence of the problem? Do they deal with the subject itself, or with external factors around him? For example, one could rather say: "I chose to take care of my children instead of leaving earlier", or "I didn't organize myself", or "I didn't prioritize this meeting". Already, something would be more internal, more related to oneself, and therefore more truthful, more authentic. But, in choosing to accuse the external, the immediate context, the surroundings, we chose to avoid including ourselves, therefore excluding our choices, our power, even our own existence.

Can our actions only be determined by an external causality? This would be a strange idea, as it would deny any autonomous power of the being. It would imply that we are only determined by an external context, by external events or factors, and therefore that the essence of what is fundamental in our existence, what generates our behavior and our actions, would rather be external, and not internal. There would thus be no freedom, since there cannot be freedom without power, freewill, and internality. Thus here arises a major problem with circumstantial thinking: it is alienated, as it externalizes the subject himself, the thinking subject, the acting subject, and deprives him of any potency, of any agency. The subject actually rejects his status of subject and makes itself an object, since it is entirely moved by outside forces. The subject is not therefore the center of his own existence, this center is situated outside of himself, he defines himself as exo-centered.

In the context of self-alienation, there is a very topical phenomenon, which can be called "economy of protocol", which replaces authenticity, risk-taking, creativity, with a technical principle or procedure, now quite popular if not obligatory in certain contexts, which gives a feeling of control and allows an evaluation with objective claims. It avoids any confrontation with oneself, by providing a rigid and "certain" framework.

It is common that whenever we want to explain ourselves, explain our mistakes or shortcomings, we naturally tend to go directly for the circumstances, rather than dealing with the grounding of the problem in ourselves. Often, our explanations start with "but it was because of …"and the explanation falls into the description of some events that are, of course, out of our control. Nevertheless, we cannot deny that there is a common denominator present in all those contextual justifications, which is the subject itself. So as much as the circumstances can be a part of reality, the subject has some part or responsibility in his actions, just as some freedom in his existence, that is not circumstantial. Indeed, existing requires responsibility, and this can not be found outside of oneself. There must be some kind of centeredness in this scattered reality. Through the externalization of the self, one negates his own being, since being is grounded in a form of interiority. The self is alienated, since it is estranged from itself, separated from its self-determination. It transfers its ownership or authority to some external power.

A problem that all circumstances have in common, is that they all propose a vision of the problem where the cause is external, instead of internal. Indeed, all above examples suggest that the problem does not come from the individual, but from an external situation that they do not control. This means that the problem is seen as coming from the outside. However, one can not disengage himself from a reality where he is engaged in, no matter if he wants it or not. This is a way of avoiding self-responsibility, and even denying one's own existence. If events always happened based on external circumstances, this would mean that the same things would happen to everybody, and would not exist according to the subject. However, we observe that A does not necessarily act like B, or that B does not think like C, and so on. This shows that there is something fundamental in one's being, such as the power of choosing, of living, of freedom and consciousness, that would be more revealing and authentic than using externality as a form of explanation.

Chapter 5

Reduction

One of the main problems of circumstantial thinking is that it is a form of reduction process. Indeed, it reduces causality to an immediate context, instead of perceiving a deeper causality, less superficial, efficient cause instead of final cause, as Aristotle would distinguish them. One way to reduce a phenomenon to circumstances is to attribute the phenomenon to a particular situation or a particular other person: "I get angry because of my wife", or "I was late today because the traffic was bad". Of course, it is possible that traffic was bad that day and that it created some delay, but we could call it a superficial causality. A deeper one, would be for example the difficulty that this person has with time or even with reality as a whole –time being one of the major features of reality –, his procrastination tendencies, or any explanation that would concern the subject and his difficulties with time. Same goes with the example of "being angry because of my wife": it is quite possible that "my wife" makes me particularly angry, it is possible that she irritates me, but this necessarily means that there is some residual anger in "me", and that "my wife" touches it in a particularly efficient way. In general, one that gets particularly or easily angry with a given person usually has anger issues in himself, as one given particular context cannot justify a repetitive reaction in our being.

Identifying circumstances can indeed be useful, to the extent we do not limit to this mere identification, that they are not exhaustive or exclusive. The mistake would be to grant them a full causal nature, which would be a reductionist understanding of the phenomenon. Circumstances should be viewed as a revelator, as a manifestation of a cause, and not as a sufficient cause in itself. We encounter here again the problem of the ambiguity of the image, being an idol or an icon, a thing in itself or a mere reflection. Taking the revelator for the cause is precisely the reductionist scheme. Therefore being angry about "my wife" shows that I have anger inside myself, otherwise "my wife" would hardly ever make me angry.

As reality englobes everything that exists, what is fundamental or necessary and what is secondary or accidental, in order for an explanation to be real or substantial, one cannot take only a unique part or factor, especially when this part or factor is a rather minimalistic one. And this would be the problem of the reduction process, what can also be called minimization: to take the secondary or accidental as the main reason, where the secondary should remain secondary, when the focus should be on the essential. Therefore when the thinking is circumstantial, the investigation of the cause, the explanation of the phenomenon doesn't deepen the issue, it remains superficial, it doesn't enter the ontological reason or nature of the process. The thinking stops at a superficial analysis, some element that more or less seems to explain or justify the problem, without entering the deeper self of the subject. Circumstantial thinking proposes a quick and easy thinking, that gets rid of the main issue, it proposes a quick and illusory solution to the problem through an avoidance strategy, by dealing with it from an external angle. Indeed, if the problem of lateness is purely one of traffic, what can we do? And what is true for external circumstances is valid as well for internal circumstances. Any analysis that occults the dimension of free-will in the explanation provides a deterministic account that can be considered reductionist, since it omits a crucial element that decided the occurrence of the phenomenon.

On the other side, we could say that taking into account the diverse circumstances that determine each thought, each word and each action denotes an awareness of the constitutive determinism of the human being. Nevertheless, this circumstantial condition should not represent an excuse to cover up one's own responsibility, being a mere observation on the order of things and self. Paradoxically, whoever knows himself as a being of circumstances frees himself at the same time from this condition, that he transcends by accepting it and by working with it, another form of responsibility and freedom. This is Spinoza's idea when he affirms that we are only free through the consciousness of our determinism.

Chapter 6

Bad faith

A strong syndrome of circumstantial thinking is the attitude of bad faith. Indeed, the person caught in the bad faith attitude doesn't want to see things as they are, doesn't want to admit them or deal with them, and prefers to deny, pretend or distort reality. A person of bad faith is a liar of a special type: a liar that tries hard to believe his lie and manages to more or less believe it, a sincere liar. Either by denying reality, or by inventing reality, to an extent that it can become pathological, mythomaniac, when consciousness tends to vanish, when such a practice becomes frequent and excessive. But common bad faith implies that we somehow know that what we say is not true, and we know that the others know it as well, although we hope to be believed. It often proceeds by merely deviating from reality or by twisting it. One must convince himself and others through different strategies. In order to justify his bad faith, he will resort to and cling to numerous secondary and irrelevant "factual" elements, to the extent they can comfort or justify his claim. We should add to our description of bad faith the Sartrian utilization of the concept. It is when someone overinvests his social role, his function or his status, believing so much in it that he restricts himself to this identity, losing sight of his fundamental existential freedom. One can say that he is totally caught up in a circumstantial world, a self-made fiction.

The one who refuses or denies ontological thinking, the one who stops himself from thinking beyond circumstances, is a person of bad faith. He will tend to be relatively conscious of such an endeavor or posture, but his denial or self-delusory capacity can lead him to become quite blind to his own reality. His main issue is often to negate his own responsibility, his own freedom, to ignore his culpability, to overlook the bearing of his own actions and choices, and the consequences deriving from it. He prefers not to see it, not to deal with it. He is in avoidance, in disavowal, he fears reality and what it would reveal of him. So, for such a person, circumstances are a real gift. They allow him to "save face" and to keep playing the "lying game", to pretend and act "as if", they feed his scheme and help him to protect it.

There are several reasons why this "bad faith" functions quite well in diverse interpersonal and social relations, which explains why circumstantial argumentation is so popular.

The first one is that it is quite a common procedure, therefore most people lack any capacity for critical thinking when they hear such speech, they are ready to credit the speaker with their trust, since they themselves would do the same, they would use the same type of arguments. Who has not used the traffic argument as a reason for being late? Therefore they do not perceive the bad faith element, they are rather gullible on this issue.

The second reason is the fear of conflict. To denounce the bad faith of someone is a risky enterprise, since we do not know how the other person would react. Most likely they are like us, they do not appreciate any suspicion or criticism, they become upset if someone doubts or denounces their words. Therefore the comfort of the social pact overrules any desire or attempt to identify the lying component of what we hear, and by dint of such a behavior we become actually blind and deaf to this type of rhetorical manipulation. Circumstantial thinking is more "human", unlike the harshness of ontological thinking, rather pitiless. So if one challenges circumstantial thinking, he will most likely be in some way ostracized for being too radical and provocative. Accepting bad faith, believing it or pretending to do so is a guarantee of social harmony, and the main ally of organized propaganda, political, religious, commercial or other.

The third one is that we prefer to see the "good" in people, with the exception of people we do not appreciate or that we envy, of course, for whom it is rather the reverse. Thus this fear of badness, a natural recoil, leads us to naively accept any speech that would occult or soften the bad intentions or the wrongdoings of a person.

The fourth one is a moral inhibition, when the circumstance has to do with some "unquestionably good" motivation, for example family issues. When someone introduces the family in his argumentation, such as "my children", his speech becomes almost sacred, since "my children" can become a justification for just about anything, that no one would dare disapprove or denounce, under the threat of being considered heartless or brutal. Strangely enough, the "good" authorizes many rhetorical tricks.

The fifth one is that there is often some truth in the circumstantial argument. Unless totally invented, it generally refers to some facts that are commonly known or reliable. As well, there is some sense in the argumentation, since those circumstances indeed can play a part in accounting for the phenomenon. We just choose to omit some more fundamental ontological dimension, which makes the isolated circumstantial argument rather conclusive.

The sixth one is the lack of self-challenge. To start challenging circumstantial thinking, one first has to avoid thinking in this fashion: to not permanently look for the comfort of self-indulgence and self-justification. Otherwise we have no reason and energy to challenge the person who indulges as well in this scheme. If I constantly look for excuses for myself, if I accept the indulgence of circumstances for my behavior, then it will not be natural for me to be demanding with someone else on this issue.

The seventh one is the complaining arrangement, the suffering pact, or the "bad luck victims club". Either we complain about the context and what was done to us, or we have to take full responsibility for our actions, and what fits for others fits for ourselves. Therefore we tend to be lenient when the others complain about circumstances, we even get a certain pleasure in comparing our circumstantial "notes" , this consoles us, all united against "fate"and the pressure of external obstacles. Lack of money, lack of time, lack of love, lack of luck, lack of recognition, misunderstanding of others, established as the reason for our difficulties are the classic complaints that bring people together and reassure them through a sense of companionship in misery.

A last feature of bad faith that seems important is the identification of phenomena as exceptions. Circumstances are supposed to be contingent, accidental, and not essential, therefore they often tend to a status of fortuity or singularity, even if it is obviously not the case. Actually, the whole point of the recourse to circumstances is to avoid any principle of necessity, of causality, of consequentiality, of responsibility. Therefore the "late person"might periodically use the traffic argument, mentioning it each time as if it was unpredictable, unfortunate and unmanageable. Consistent patterns are prohibited, that would make us responsible since there is coherence in the world, therefore events have to remain exceptional, even if it is obviously not the case. That is why the word "sometimes" is so popular, as a way to avoid any categorical or probable statement or consideration, considered more compromising. The "once", the "only today", the "exceptionally", by making the event rare and dramatic, unplanned and extraordinary, reinforces the argument through some emotional content, making it more operational and credible. As well, the exceptional dimension of a wrongdoing makes it more pardonable, since viewed as a mere accident, in a way disconnected from the "usual person", of which the cause is attributed to external circumstances, identifiable or mysterious. Therefore we can oppose bad faith to authenticity: the one that hides in circumstances is not authentic, since he doesn't embrace reality and is not in accordance with himself.

Chapter 7

Victimization

Based on the same phenomenon described above on the externalization of the subject, another issue is the position taken by the subject, in his relation to reality. For in circumstantial thinking, instead of taking a responsible, autonomous and noble posture, one takes a victim position, a suffering, submissive and impotent attitude. One becomes a victim of circumstances, a victim of the world, and strangely enough even a victim of himself. The individual is not in control anymore, he is no longer responsible for the events that occur, he remains in a weak and passive position. He gives up on his freedom, out of choice of ease or comfort, out of weakness, he is no longer an agent of his own existence, he does not embrace the power of his being. The victim doesn't have any energy, any strength: the victim suffers from outside powers, from fate, from his executioners. The victim is usually conscious about being a victim, he in fact claims this status, although he might not dare to explicitly name it, thus he tends to lessen, or even eliminate what does not fit this scheme. The victim, being a victim in his own eyes, eliminates for himself all possibility of freedom. That is why he is so interested and even obsessed with circumstances, which so gracefully and generously justify this victim status.

Sometimes, we can call ourselves victims for sound reasons. In fact we are always the victim of something, since in large parts we do not choose the nature of the context we live in. Although we can always modify at least some aspects of our life and our environment, and especially we can modify our reading of the context we are plunged into, modify our attitude. But often, to be a victim tends to become a role, a choice of the partition we wish to play in life. The victim of circumstantial thinking plays the role of a powerless creature, tossed about by the vagaries of the contingencies of the world, on which he has little or no control. Again, one can feel like a victim for some sound reasons, but still, it is a chosen attitude, never an obligation or a necessity. Our existence is in essence not accidental, as much as accidents can of course happen and do happen constantly, and they affect us.

Everyday, every hour, we choose our own existence by taking actions upon the world and ourselves, by thinking, and even by deciding to remain alive. Even if we consider that our birth is not our choice, our life depends on our choices, being determined by our decisions, our initiatives, our thoughts, our behaviors, etc., which largely depend on our will. By being in a state of victimhood, we don't embrace our existence, we escape our responsibility, our choices, and the power inherent to life as a human being. It is a way to be complacent with ourselves, in order not to be confronted to the abyss of our being, to the darkness of our soul. It is so much easier to blame the neighbor, the traffic, or even God, who too often seems to do things despite common sense.

One of the basic assumptions of numerous schools of wisdom is that happiness is not circumstantial. Being happy does not depend on any external element, but only on the disposition of the subject, his personal paradigm, his ability to play with his representations, his moral strength. The philosophical subject is in this sense the co-author of his own circumstances. He recuperates all the circumstances in order to turn them into foes or allies, or remain indifferent to them. Therefore no circumstantial excuse is valid in order to justify our actions or our mental state. In this sense, circumstantial thinking is anti-philosophical, since it places the subject in the position of victim of the world.

We should as well tackle briefly the problem of self-victimhood, when we are in our own eyes a victim of ourselves. This phenomenon takes place when we attribute to ourselves a determined nature, an essence, a fixed character, when we explain our behavior through some past events of our lives. Of course, we can admit that we have a certain personality with given limits and shortcomings, given gifts and handicaps. But two other features are necessary to become a victim of this reality. The first one is a certain passivity, when we take for granted this "nature" of ours, when we reify it or absolutize it, when we do not struggle with it at all, when we let our inclinations or tendencies totally take over our being, what can be called complacency. The second one is when we develop a certain resentment towards our own self, our own limits, just like we would do against some bully bothering our daily life, inducing a suffering and complaining attitude, instead of reconciling with our own reality, accepting the finitude of being. Those are the two general conditions for the process of self-victimhood.

Kierkegaard, one of the fathers of existentialism, argued that it is the act of making choices that brings meaning to our lives. Through making choices, we live authentically, forming our own opinions, rather than being guided by the opinions of others or by society. We can think that this applies to the circumstances as well. Being guided and determined by circumstances would make a thinking and acting subject transforming into a poor sheep, and would keep his life from having any meaning, any authenticity. This is what we call the phenomenon of victimization, wherever the bully is oneself, the world, the society, others, or the traffic.

Chapter 8

Complacency

Justifying our actions, our difficulties, or some schemes, through circumstances, engenders a tendency of complacency, of self-satisfaction, even if this self-satisfaction is quite superficial and fake. Indeed, by using circumstances to define a behavior, one does not question his being, his choices, his attitude, since he uses scattered elements that are outside of his power in order to justify himself. The complacent subject chooses to ignore any problem or difficulty that he might have with himself, and instead chooses to see what he wants to see, what is more comfortable.

In circumstantial thinking, there is no work on the self, one doesn't try to improve, to get better, to understand how he functions or even how the world functions, since fortuity runs things. Such an individual develops a tendency to think that things are the way they are, and that it is. There is no critical thinking, no problematization of one's being, nor a mise en abyme of the self. The pitfall is that it creates a form of dependence on external sources that do not belong to him or concern him directly. With this mode of thinking, there is neither the need nor the desire to see how one's own way of being can be part of the ongoing phenomenon, which leads to an impasse. Circumstantial thinking brings about a superficial relation to oneself and to the world, that will work for all complacent suiters that are not interested in confrontation nor challenging their vision of the world.

To restrict oneself to a circumstantial paradigme reveals little or no interest in fundamental causes and global processes, a lack of curiosity and motivation to modify reality, since one remains in the superficial and the predetermined. It shows a certain ease in accepting any argument or reason as valid without much critical evaluation, it manifests a certain difficulty in confronting people and ideas, some impotence with oneself or others. It is simpler and more comfortable, since we avoid digging into the complexity and contemplating the whole. Who knows what could be found in those somber places...

As part of the principle of complacency, we should introduce the concept of habit. Although we could have also introduced it as part of victimhood, since quite often people justify their actions and behaviors through this idea of habit as some unchangeable feature of themselves in which they are caught as in a rigid existential trap, therefore being a victim of themselves. But it can also be taken as a form of complacency, since the subject confuses cause and consequence, taking the latter as the former. Often, when people are asked why they do something problematic, for example when they have some type of unhealthy addiction, they answer: "It is because of habit". As we just explained, the habit is a consequence, not a cause, although this consequence has taken a life of its own, carrying its own energy it weighs with its own inertia. Therefore, when we explain a situation with the concept of habit, we refuse or avoid going back to the original source of the problem, to rethink the moment where we sort of took the decision to fall into this "habit", actively or passively, consciously or unconsciously. Rather than reexamining the moment of "freedom", we prefer to acknowledge the situation we are enclosed in as a self-evident fact, almost as some essential or unchangeable part of our being. This apathy or indolence, this fatalist acceptance of a made up "reality" can indeed be called complacency, since there is no self-challenge or self-consciousness. We should add that habit can as well be a positive and useful practice, when it reinforces a power of being, when it is useful, when it ritualizes a creative or productive activity, when it helps in taking up a challenge. Then it does not inhibit, it allows or facilitates. But such a habit generally implies a certain effort in order to be maintained, it is not complacent. Therefore, the "habit" justification is part of circumstantial thinking mainly when it is used to justify an unhealthy practice. A habit becomes circumstantial thinking when one doesn't question it anymore, when it becomes automatic, when we ignore its nature and its consequences, when it justifies a problematic behavior, and is then used to deny any sense of freedom or responsibility.

Chapter 9

Self-protection

The world can be a harsh place, human beings are often merely trying to survive, attempting to protect themselves within this difficult context, protecting themselves from such a context. They try to obtain their minimal share of happiness, or at least temporary pleasure, and thus make their way through life in an acceptable way. Commonly, besides what they perceive as obligations, people are primarily motivated by their own desires and needs. Hippocrate said: "Desperate times call for desperate measures". And who or what is more desperate than a human being trying to survive through life? One can lie, cheat or betray, in order to survive. This is already the case for material preoccupations, it is even more the case for psychological ones, like the ambition to be recognized by others or mere self-acceptance in relation to oneself. Thus, one will naturally practice circumstantial thinking. Blame the others, blame the world, blame the traffic in order to "feel better"with oneself and the society. Hide through externality in order to survive internally.

It is true that it is not easy to confront oneself with reality, especially when we realize it is the source of much suffering. We already have to deal with the chaos of the world, so, as much as possible, we try to avoid dealing with our own. What is interesting to observe, is that in reality, the main source of suffering would rather be ourselves, as we produce in our life a little world that is flawed and fragile. We produce fantasies in our mind, diverse illusions, which we sincerely believe in, or that we want to believe, but that can be eliminated so quickly and easily. Especially by others, those who observe us with a critical eye, who often perceive us better than ourselves. Already we see why, circumstantially, it seems that others are the actual source of our suffering: as others, as outside observers, they are a danger, they represent a threat. A threat to our little world, to our intimacy, to our little bubble, and we must protect ourselves from such strangers. Not letting them intrude too much, in order to avoid their judgment, their disagreement, or any form of obstacle from their side. In such cases, circumstances can be used as a way to protect ourselves, by giving us excuses that would avoid confrontation with others, or with ourselves. The principle is that circumstances are often something external, that usually belong to the category of "out of control", therefore nothing can be done against them, they are apparently sturdy. Circumstantial arguments maintain a superficial foundation that prevents any confrontation or deep analysis of the other. How can others understand and judge our actions if they do not fall under our responsibility? "It was not my fault, I am a victim of reality."If we examine this circumstantial reaction, what can we see? We observe that there is a desire to justify ourselves, to exempt ourselves from any liability, and to protect ourselves from any terrible accusation that would say: "This is your fault, therefore you are bad!"In such cases, circumstantial thinking, whether it is conscious or not –often it is not –maintains some kind of protective cape, where one is not really responsible for his life, therefore we cannot be judged by our deeds.

Chapter 10

Easiness

Circumstantial thinking, unlike ontological thinking, has numerous advantages; among others, it is quite accessible, easy and popular. Indeed, everyone can look at the circumstances, everyone does it naturally, as they are surrounding us, as they appear rather visibly. It is the surface, the top, the tangible, the tip of the iceberg. Everybody has an eye on it, it is difficult to miss it or to deny it. Unlike the ontological thinking that is underneath, more invisible and harder to reach, one has to really look for it. That is why it is so obvious for people to share circumstances, to have a common usage of them, a common understanding of them. Everyone is familiar with circumstances, the majority constantly refers to them. Everybody knows what a circumstance is, even though most people call it "reality" rather than "circumstance", since it is endowed with a strong and reliable nature. Everybody "knows", or at least can concede, that traffic is an acceptable argument to justify arriving late to a meeting.

There is something popular about it, as we can notice that similar circumstances are used everywhere, a sort of innate common sense. People accept each other's justification, it is a conventional explanation, grasped and recognized by the majority. All individuals have a history, a background, and they identify themselves to it, they easily refer to it, and they naturally use it to explain their own behaviors and actions. We all have good reasons to not be what we could be or what we should be. On the other hand, we need courage in order to think ontologically. It is more challenging, a characteristic which explains why so often it is not chosen. Such an interpretation requires being bold, being thoughtful, and being willing to look at oneself.

An example of this easiness is visible today through the common use of psychological concepts and explanations. Freudian determinism, largely introjected in Western civilization, explains to us that each subject is the product of family circumstances that have determined what he is. This idea is attractive because it makes the subject less responsible, since each of us would be condemned by the circumstances that forged him to be what he is. Thus everyone has some little stories of the past that can thus explain his actions and behaviors, and one does not have to go further in his explanations. Of course, one omits that there remains a fundamental freedom, what can be called the choice of the narration: how we tell this event, how we relate to it. Any incident can be told as a dramatic event, as a comic event, as an absurd event, as an insignificant event, as something that reveals others more than it reveals ourselves, etc. But in order to accomplish such a deliberate transvaluation, we need the work of consciousness, of reflection, of willpower.

Chapter 11

Procrastination

Procrastination is an interesting form of circumstantial thinking, which has to do with both time and conditions. It takes two different forms, in relation to the present and in relation to the future. First, it criticizes or negates the present, which is of course rarely appropriate or satisfying. The actual circumstances are never right: we do not have enough time, the situation is not opportune, the context is not conducive to our activity or our decisions, we are not psychologically ready, we lack inspiration, we are tired or we lack energy, we have other priorities, etc. Second, it overinvests the future, be it tomorrow or most likely some indeterminate ulterior moment, a time to come where everything will rightly fall into place. These future circumstances, often mysterious, embody or represent our hopes, our expectations, sometimes our wildest imagination, providing the ground for some naive optimism or even enchantment, unlike the sad and powerless present. The better tomorrows, the future paradise, what is called in French "the tomorrows that sing", for they seduce us with their idyllic and charming refrains. In the future, everything becomes possible, since no obstacles impose themselves de facto on our mirific and cloudless horizon. We just forget that we carry with ourselves our own fabricated circumstances, our very personal way to systematically find reasons not to do things and to feel impotent, falling short of any self-accomplishment. The future has no reason to get it.

Through external or internal circumstances, numerous persons are quite tempted or eager to abandon their freedom and remain heteronomous, they have a hard time to take decisions and to follow up on them. But instead of facing their own self and its natural inclinations, they easily fall back on those common justifications in order to avoid any self-challenge. In this sense we could say that procrastination represents a fear of the ontological experience. The sense of void and indetermination, the vertigo provoked by the mise en abyme of the self. We rather chose the option of the immediate, the urgent instead of the important, the superficial constraint, internal or external, instead of the ontological demand of self-accomplishment. Which is why procrastinators are often last-minute adepts, they delay as much as possible the adventure. They rely on the context, they want to be forced to do things, rather than exercise the frightening power of freedom.

Chapter 12

Neediness

Another manifestation of circumstantial thinking is the psychological phenomenon of neediness, indirectly connected to the idea of victimhood, since we undergo this need, even if it is self-imposed. As we have seen, the CT grants enormous importance to external events and to internal ones, more than to his personal freedom. He has strong expectations, and a high degree of sensitivity, which combine in a form of addiction, of dependency. More than wanting a "this or that", he needs a "this or that", a necessity and a satisfaction on which depends his well-being, his achievement, his self-recognition, etc. As examples of such necessities, we need food or shelter in order to survive materially, emotional support or recognition in order to find some psychological stability, drama or excitement in order to avoid boredom, a vocation or a function in order to avoid meaninglessness, an identity or status in order to exist or have personal significance, etc. Such necessities can be basic, reasonable, others are more personal or social artificial mental constructions, more or less arbitrary, more or less legitimate, more or less temperate.

A need is an internal sense of obligation –even when it is related to the outside –, a necessity, we require something, someone, some event, some status, not just because they would be pleasant or useful, not merely because we would like to obtain them, but because they are considered essential, necessary or very important. To a large extent, we consider we cannot exist without this contentment; in its absence, life would be unbearable. Therefore, the person who is bound to a need denies his fundamental freedom, his power to make decisions autonomously or rationally, his free-will, since it strongly limits its possibility of reason and action. As soon as an obstacle appears to prevent the satisfaction of this need, when a difficulty or problem imposes itself, the subject suffers and becomes obsessive. When he feels stuck, he naturally expects help from others, he becomes a beggar, an expectation which adds weight on the load of his needs. He will feel impotent, and he justifies his "begging"with the idea that he is not prepared, powerful, mature, intelligent or lucky enough to find solutions by himself. He will become anxious, angry or resentful. He can be envious, since the others, those who are "satisfied", seem to be better off or more powerful. The needy person easily sees himself as someone helpless, like a child. And the others can be perceived as his potential "saviors", "betrayers"or even "persecutors", although these relations are reversible, since there are different ways to need others: some people as well need to save or persecute.

Part II:

The imposture syndrome

God then said: "We have given you, Adam, no fixed seat nor
features proper to yourself nor endowment peculiar to you alone,
in order that whatever seat, whatever features, whatever
endowment you may responsibly desire, these same you may have
and possess according to your desire and judgment. Once defined,
the nature of all other beings is constrained within the laws
prescribed by us. You, on the contrary, constrained by no limits,
may determine it for yourself, according to your own free will, in
whose hand we have placed you. I have placed you at the world's
center so that you may thence more easily look around at whatever
is in the world. We have made you neither of heaven nor of earth,
neither mortal nor immortal, so that you may, as the free and
extraordinary shaper of yourself, fashion yourself in the form you
prefer. It will be in your power to degenerate into the lower forms
of life, which are brutish; you shall have the power, according to
your soul's judgment, to be reborn into the higher orders, which
are divine".

Oration on the Dignity of Man
Pico della Mirandola

Chapter 1

Circumstantial imposture

Imposture seems to be a crucial human characteristic. Beasts don't display such a feature, they simply are what they are. A priori gods and angels should not suffer from this fate, although various myths recount exceptions to such a principle. For example the most beautiful angel Lucifer, the light bearer, rebelling against God, resentful not to be granted what he thought he deserved, deprived of what he thought he was in his own right, to be the favorite of the Almighty, thus becoming the devil. Another example is the Judgment of Paris, a contest between the three most beautiful goddesses of Olympus: Aphrodite, Hera and Athena, for the prize of a golden apple addressed to the "Fairest of them all", a contest that turned out badly and caused the bloody Trojan wars: each goddess pretended to represent "true beauty", in opposition to the others. For the Greeks, in the cosmos every being has its place, every being should know and occupy its lawful setting, and not pretend to some higher status. But of course, man is condemned to be free, as Sartre wrote. And this freedom naturally leads to pretension, to excessive claims, to illegitimate and senseless yearnings. We aspire to the absolute, to the divine, to the transcendence, what can be called the human genius. And in this sense we somewhat have access to the unconditional, we experience it, ephemerally, partially, limitedly. But at the same time, the aspirations are never far from the claims, and that is where the imposture starts. We believe we have arrived, that we are there, that we have it, that we are this or that, that we have reached the mountain top. Thus we want to stay there and benefit from the status and the advantages, we give up any "superfluous" climbing. And since it is hard to anchor and maintain this belief, too many features of reality undermine it, we strive for some types of acknowledgements, recognitions or else, in order to feed our insatiable and imposible desire to believe.

An impostor is a person who pretends to be someone else than he is in order to deceive others, and probably himself, generally in the perspective of a fraudulent gain. This gain is generally connected to getting love, recognition, fame, status, or some practical advantage. What we call the "impostor syndrome" is characterized by the feeling, legitimate or not, of being a fraud. It indicates in a subject the sentiment of being an existential fake. This impression is generally felt as an unpleasant experience, since it implies a certain degree of discomfort and alienation from oneself, a deep sensation of dissatisfaction. The problem for the impostor is that he condemns himself to a certain blindness for his scheme to really function: he has to exert all his efforts in order to ignore or deny his own mental state and psychological functioning, in order to cover up his profound internal discrepancy. Even though, of course, he will not be able to totally curtail the jolts and somersaults of his consciousness.

We should as well mention that the term syndrome contains a certain ambiguity. For one, it indicates a set of physical or psychological conditions showing that one has a particular disease or pathology. On the other hand, it indicates a set of opinions or a way of behaving that is typical of a particular type of person, a given attitude. In the former, one is suffering from the syndrome, as a powerless victim, in the latter, it can be a choice, willingly and consciously determined. And it seems to us that this ambiguity should remain, since being an impostor can indeed be freely chosen, but as we will describe it, it is as well part of the human condition and the result of a given individual existential past, with a significant unconscious dimension.

We will distinguish two types of such impostors: the circumstantial one, and the ontological one.

The circumstantial imposter undergoes the experience of imposture, he suffers from this psychological complex for personal historical reasons. The basic dynamic of it is often connected to receiving frequent high praise, generally in childhood, which indirectly inculcated a strong ego ideal, a high idea of the self, and at the same time a permanent doubt about the reality or possibility of this "greatness". Thus he is the best, the first, the only, the unique, and without realizing it he becomes the navel of the world.

Simultaneously, one receives an assertion of greatness, an obligation of greatness, accompanied by a constant insecurity about the reality of this greatness. Thus, parents who keep excessively praising their children under the guise of boosting their self-confidence produce at the same time an ambitious ego ideal and the fear of failing for not being up to the mark. The anxiety is inevitable, since the objective reality of diverse experiences will permanently remind the growing child that he is not up to par in relation to what he was told, since he will obviously periodically fail expectations or meet people who are better than he is in whatever competition he feels engaged in. And any accomplishment will find him anyhow unsatisfied, any success will always be considered insufficient in the light of his high ambitions. More perversely, as time goes, any confirmation of his greatness will always be received with a high degree of suspicion, since this person has developed the strong and rational belief that he was initially lied to. More dramatically, such a person can develop the idea that he does not deserve to be loved, since the love he initially received was based on an illusion or a scam, or was itself an illusion or scam. Therefore, when he receives attestation of love from someone else, he will either think it cannot last since the "lover"is being fooled and he will necessarily be disillusioned at some point. Or the subject will suspect this "lover" cannot be truthful, he is just trying to manipulate him in order to obtain something suspicious or illicit. Therefore the "impostor"lives a life of fear, instability and insecurity, where everyone is involved in some manipulatory scheme, where one can only be disappointed or deceived. As well, as a child with his parents, when facing the manifestation of love or recognition, there will be the contradictory attitude of being satisfied with this attestation, and being dissatisfied, angry or even scornful toward those who are engaged in this operation of deceit, because they are either lying or being merely stupid if they are sincere in their approval or affection. The poor lover will therefore not understand the shift in moods of the impostor he loves, remaining puzzled or shocked by his unpredictable irritation or anger. The subject is in fact convinced that he is merely playing a role of "greatness" , just pretending, as an actor would do, or the way children play doctor or teacher. Alternatively, he will go along with it, acting proud or arrogant, ceaselessly trying to show or prove his greatness, often overplaying it, what can be called the manic side, or he will be exhausted from this permanent game of perception and calculations, he will give up and yield to what he considers the reality, thus ceding to depression or resentment. One can lament that parents ignore this phenomenon, but we should understand that the poor parents have a hard time relinquishing the idea that their child is the eighth wonder of the world, for their own existential reasons: he is their ultimate chance of greatness.

To conclude this general presentation, let us say that anger is a dominant feature of the circumstantial impostor, a characteristic that is quite understandable. After all, such an individual goes out of his way to produce an image, to prove to himself and others what he is, or rather what he would like to be, but his efforts easily feel threatened, the slightest gust of wind threatens his house of cards, primarily because he himself does not really believe his own elaboration. Without realizing it - it would be too painful to do so - he fears the slightest suspicion of being a fraud, the mere expressed or alluded inkling of not being for real; any comment or behavior can be perceived as a threat to his existential efforts. He even gets extremely sensitive or paranoid about other people's reactions, overestimating their content and their intention, what can be called heightened sensitivity. This goes both for criticism and for compliments, since he is quite keen on hearing the latter, craving for anything cozying up, flattering or confirming his desired image. This is quite noticeable for example in the academic world, where those rituals of appreciative and obsequious speeches are a loaded obligation. Any breach in such a formality is easily perceived as a humiliating attack, even the most subtle perception of transgression is taken as a declaration of war. Therefore anger, like boiling lava waiting under a volcano, always threatens to burst out, manifesting an intense existential pain. The circumstantial impostor invests heavily in otherness, he tremendously relies on it, he overinvests in the exterior, he overextends himself by trying to reach some impossible satisfaction, as a compensation of an internal abyss he prefers to ignore, of an anguish that can never be quenched. He is an eternal beggar. Thus, he can never be satisfied, he is too greedy, he is asking too much, from which comes the disappointment, the depression, the anger.

The circumstantial impostor lives in delusion, feeding himself on his fantasms. He indulges in a periodic regretful wishful thinking. He easily thinks "I could have done X if…", "I could have been Y if ⋯" He indulges in the contemplation of an overinflated self, rather unjustified. Outside events and obstacles are the reasons for his nonrealization. His being needs no actualization in order to be great: he is great just because he is who he is, just because he feels he is great, without having to accomplish anything. Of course, he does not fundamentally believe in this greatness, since it is a shallow "make believe", thus he constantly seeks the comfort of compliments, and fears those criticisms that would remind him of his own doubts. This explains why he takes everything personally, since the center of his world is his little person, impregnated or saturated with its illusions, therefore permanently needy. Circumstantial people get offended. They get angry, they are disgusted, they feel envy, they undergo frustration, too many parameters go easily awry, too many expectations are betrayed. They are not detached from the empirical. And when they manage some detachment, they are not detached from the detachment: they need it too much, so they search for circumstances in order to encounter detachment and protect it. Some activity, some commitment, some ritual that would allow them to escape reality.

Another typical scheme of CI rests on The fear of idiocy, the fear of being stupid or looking stupid. Some persons will more or less live with this feeling of stupidity, remaining rather withdrawn. But some others decide to put on a show, they seriously invest in the production of a smart looking image, which can be done in many different ways. One can be learned, cunning, funny, manipulative, ambitious, critical or provocative.The activity displayed in order to look smart can even be an actual "smart"activity, even though this person has the suspicion or the belief of "in reality"not being smart. It would almost look like the OI, since there is a sort of ideal. But there is a big difference: the CI does not accept within himself and in the eyes of others his own insufficiencies, real or imaginary; he is busy hiding them, denying them, it would be very difficult for him to admit his suspected or actual idiocy. Thus he fears any exposure or denunciation of his shortcomings. This makes him anxious, sensitive, susceptible. In an ironic way, he puts on a show because he is convinced he must put on a show, although it is not a show: he is actually trying to survive, he is risking his neck in such an enterprise.

Although there are two types of reaction to this fear of idiocy. The manic modality, where one would react dynamically to this fear: those will read, study, gather information, trying to get smarter and show their smartness, always ready to compete and fight in the presence of any threat. And the depressive modality, more passive, of those who do not have the energy or are not willing to exert themselves in order to compensate for their shortcomings or create some illusion. They merely oscillate between the expression of anger and the sad admittance of their idiocy. But they all watch the gaze of others, the primary form of alienation and imposture.

The circumstantial impostor tends to take things personally. Ideas are always addressed to him as a person, with explicit or hidden private messages, more likely "negative". He cannot receive information or ideas in a detached fashion, he cannot contemplate a mere phenomenon as some interesting, or not interesting data. Therefore he will not analyze the content objectively, he will not listen to the speech or perceive the action in themselves, he is too needy for this. He has too many expectations, therefore he will perceive things in relation to his wants and lacks, as much as what he perceives can satisfy or frustrate them. And of course this biased subjective outlook will as well affect his understanding and acceptance of individuals. He will easily inscribe them in categories that he considers positive or negative, in a very shallow and immediate way, short circuiting any real substantial and challenging thinking process. "What's in it for me"is the underlying leitmotif of his mental attitude, a very reductioning worldview. For example, he cannot stand when someone tells him what to do, even a simple recommandation, since he will view such an injunction from the outside as demeaning or insulting, he will feel infantilized, treated as an inferior or as an object. If he had sufficient distance and objectivity, he would rationally and peacefully examine this instruction or this suggestion, peacefully examining them, instead of instinctively and nervously rejecting them. But unless the subject maintains himself in a self-challenging askesis modality of being, any incitement to act or think from the outside will just remind the subject of his worthless identity. Thus challenging comments will be felt as painful and threatening, or as despotic and arbitrary. Any appeal to his consciousness or his reason will be considered intrusive and aggressive. Mentioning his problems or difficulties will never be welcomed, will never be taken as a gesture of assistance. He is so fragile, one has to be nice with him, he is eager to receive compliments.

Blaise Pascal addresses as well the issue of imposture through the principle of a "double thinking". To explain it, he tells the story of a castaway taken for their king by the people of an island where he fortuitously landed. This man becomes king by chance, following a mistake by the inhabitants of the island who have lost their sovereign. The anecdote illustrates the contingency of our condition: nothing justifies our privileges, our rank, our function, not even our birth or our existence, which are not necessary, which are in fact the results of accidental events. Although the man accepts to enter the game, to play his conventional role, he remains conscious that his kingship does not belong to him by any right, his power and his kingdom are not owed to him, they do not belong to his being. One should not confuse his social condition and his true being, his role and his self, his image and his intimate person: in a way, any manner of being is always an imposture, especially if we identify with it, if we think it is our nature or essence. He was inspired by Montaigne who wrote: "We have to play our role properly, but as the role of a borrowed character. Of the mask and the appearance one must not make a real essence, nor of the foreign to us make one's own peculiarity." Therefore we have our social thinking, inviting us to play our role as well as possible, and our intimate thinking, our hidden reflection and consciousness: we must not be fooled by our social role in our inner self. Such a principle is encountered later on in the "bad faith" of Sartre: we must not get caught up in the functioning of our empirical self, we must identify to the freedom of the transcendental self, our fundamental undetermined identity. Zhuangzi addresses the same issue by claiming that the only real self of any person is the Dao, the universal cosmic principle, anything else is insubstantial and ephemeral, corrupted by "intention". The consequence of such a phenomenon, since our mind cannot remain fully unconscious, is that we are always suspicious of the fraudulent dimension of our own existence. Therefore any attempt to "truly believe" in our formal and social identity will result in a permanent anxiety, in a constant quest for some confirmation of a borrowed identity, loose and unstable, that we cannot fundamentally trust. A chronic deception that can account well for human misery.

From this perspective, we can envisage the hypothesis that a large part of human speech is a manipulation attempt: most of the time, when we express ourselves, it is geared toward obtaining something for ourselves. In other words, speech is always performative, it is an action upon the world, articulated with a specific purpose. We can identify the few main classical goals behind the speech. To obtain material advantages of different kinds, to be recognized, accepted or admired, to be appreciated or loved, to control or to hold power, to obtain and maintain a social status. Overall, we can see this in good part as a desire for polymorphous reassurance about our own imposture. Without forgetting the expression of anxiety about not obtaining what we expect, and the manifestation of anger and envy when we do not get it. Altogether, we can call it a desire for survival, be it biological or psychological, social or symbolical. The only escape from such a "theater" is what fundamentally belongs to humanity: the exercise of reason and the expression of creativity. Be it to modify or understand reality, through an artistic, intellectual or scientific work, by searching and expressing the truth, by playing with the world and with oneself, altogether what expresses freedom, joy and beauty. Such a drive is an end in itself, and not the means of another end. There can still be a kind of manipulation in such a context, because the articulation of speech remains an exercise of power, conscious or not. But this manipulation is deliberate, it is oriented towards an enhancement of the individual and of humanity as a whole, towards the expression of his nobility and his freedom. Although often such loftier activities can be mixed with the previous survival category. We can observe this mix of genres for example when the beauty of speech is used as a tool for deception, when science is constrained to its functional dimension, when philosophy is reduced to an academic exercise, when artistic work becomes a quest for glory. Totally freeing oneself from an instinctive desire to personally survive is a rather difficult endeavor, since the human remains in spite of all an animal.

The human being often needs circumstances to act, as Nietzsche criticized, he is reactive rather than active, whether in the field of ideas or in the face of events. As a result, we can say that he is not really free, even if he reacts as he wills, or rather as he feels. He lacks energy, for lack of project or ontological direction, his passions are quite passive. Because he often lacks that internal and autonomous movement that characterizes a free existence, he depends on the outside, and on its own uncontrolled and arbitrary moods. He enjoys disagreeing, without much analysis or argumentation, because it cheaply provides him with a sense of identity, a feeling of being different and unique.

Chapter 2

Arrogance

Arrogance is one of the most common manifestations of the impostor syndrome. The arrogant person is one who has haughty and insolent manners, excessively so, lacking basic respect and recognition for others. Such a behavior reveals an exaggerated sense of one's own importance, status or abilities. But there again, we maintain the hypothesis that such a person cannot constantly, really and doubtlessly believe what he is trying to show or prove. Either because willy-nilly reason cannot be stopped and accomplishes its critical work within the mind of the subject, even unconsciously, or because diverse events and phenomena take care of undermining such wishful thinking. With any slight psychological distance this internal reality will be obvious to the external observer, but most people being themselves affected by internal discrepancies and lack of trust in themselves, what is commonly called "lack of self-confidence", will miss the point when confronted with the arrogant individual. They will inadvertently credit his outward behavior, they will take it at face value because they will feel hurt or insulted: it will activate and reveal their own insecurities, therefore granting power to the arrogant individual, who badly needs to be believed by others since he has doubts about himself. In fact, people with low self-esteem will be the unconscious accomplices of the arrogant, and the system will be self-sustaining.

If he is told, the imposter will deny his own arrogance, since it is too difficult for him to recognize it, psychologically and cognitively. But there is a tragic irony: those around him can see that the arrogance thinly veils the need to prove, to himself and others, that he is worthy of his own self-respect and their respect. As we already said, this fighting, this survival mode is clearly visible to those capable of looking, for those who know how to look. Although, if for common sense it is obvious that under such a display of "confidence"this person has some difficulties with himself, those who are caught in their own fears and preoccupations will easily miss this dimension. Therefore, arrogance is for this reason a strategy of preemption: one acts arrogant as an attempt to hide one's weakness and failure, an important feature of the imposter syndrome. Putting down others is therefore an important part of trying to emerge, as one cannot naturally and confidently stand above others, as he in fact is suspicious about himself. Thus, the most tempting strategy of the arrogant, his trademark, is to lower others, gratuitously, systematically.

Here, we should distinguish confidence and arrogance, which are easily confused, by both the actor and by the observer. As a first comment we should state that the confident person is at ease with himself, he is rather at peace and joyful, he can be friendly and empathetic, at least he is concerned with others. As well, the confident person looks for trustworthy interlocutors, and he will respect them. If you feel good about yourself, you want a good sparring partner for dialogue, just like in martial arts, you want to be challenged and dealing with a strong partner is more joyful, more risky, more interesting. Without despising an inexperienced interlocutor, with whom it will be necessary to show patience and understanding, another form of askesis, work on oneself and perseverance. An insecure person is not animated by joy; he is not preoccupied with intellectual interest or with being challenged, since his main preoccupation is protecting his own identity, to promote himself. His ideal situation of interaction is not actual exchange with others, but to defeat them, and the weaker the other person is, the higher the chances are to win. Because to win is to gain affirmation. Thus he has to browbeat his interlocutor, or even humiliate him. With arrogance, one has to "show" others, the subject needs to be "seen" in order for himself to be convinced, since he has a hard time believing his own worth. Arrogance is a feeling of superiority, or a wish of superiority, coupled with fear, with strong insecurity and doubt. That is why the arrogant posture takes on exaggerated forms, in order to make one's worth more visible, more confirmed. It is only through the eyes of the other that the arrogant can receive validation, in order to be able to believe in the image he has constructed for himself. But the image is fragile, it is in permanent need of reaffirmation from the other to continue existing in its exaggerated, bloated state.

Even if what the arrogant claims is relatively true, that he is superior in some aspect to the other person he speaks to, the mere fact that he undergoes the need to express it at the expense of his interlocutor, who might be hurt or humiliated, reveals a profound weakness of the self, a narcissistic wound, a painful crevice in the soul. He is like a child bragging to his friends, a sort of egotistic complacency. Therefore, objectively, whatever superiority he is claiming is actually undermined or annihilated by his superficial need for ostentatiously displaying himself, his need for peacocking. Although the problem for the listener is to assess if what seems like arrogance is actually a neurotic and compulsive behavior, or if it is rather the expression of a true self-confidence, free and joyful. But like we have said before, if the observer himself is anxious about his own self, he will not be able to make such judgment and assess the difference: he will be too preoccupied with his own inadequacies.

A rather ironic dimension of the arrogant impostor can be called the "scared and scary" pattern, rather paradoxical. Basically, such a person will take on a rather stern, passive aggressive, formal, somber or unsympathetic persona. He will tend to scare his interlocutors, they will naturally avoid him, but they will often ignore the fact that he is actually scared by them, unless they are rather clear and self-conscious, in the philosophical positive sense of the expression, meaning to be aware of one's identity, power and limitations. Dealing with others provokes anxiety in the arrogant soul, he is always afraid to be rejected, undervalued or scorned, thus any encounter is for him perilous and should be avoided. His unfriendly attitude seems to indicate a sense of superiority, but as always, such a pretentious behavior indicates a troubled psyche. Both relation to himself and to others are painful, since he is haunted by a sense of personal worthlessness. Thus he puts on an appearance that will unconsciously guarantee that others remain at bay, even though he will in fact suffer from such isolation, reinforcing his existential drama. His desire to be scary will be proportional to his own fear, although most likely he will not realize it, such an awareness being obviously too scary.

Chapter 3

Addiction

One noticeable aspect of the circumstantial impostor syndrome we should mention before moving on is the addictive dimension of the phenomenon. Faced with his own meaninglessness or nothingness, the person who undergoes an impostor feeling permanently "needs" – although it can be called an acquired taste – the reiteration of those words and actions that were the initial cause of his problem, just like with a drug addiction. Even though, like in drug dependency, the subject can remain rather conscious of the pathological or illusory dimension of this addiction. It is possible that in growing up, he recognized the unhealthy relationship and matured out of it; yet any source of flattery or a potential one might easily reawaken the addiction. He needs the soothing caress of those words that made him feel great and wonderful, he needs to hear the confirmation of his own worth, to hear the praise of his deeds, the value of his being, a very narcissistic form of requirement. The more he feels worthless, the more he needs the confirmation, but the more he obtains this confirmation, the more he will become suspicious of it, will get bored and feel worthless.

At the same time, those with imposter syndrome give power by default to those who give them any attention, since they are craving this attention. That is how they can as well get manipulated, for diverse reasons. Either because the praiser consciously wants to obtain something from his victim, a basic manipulatory technique, in seduction for example, or simply because the praiser himself has a compulsive need: the need to be needed, what can be called codependency. This phenomenon is common in familial relations, between parents and children, or within a couple. As well, by praising "our own", we are indirectly praising ourselves. Thus this addiction often starts very early, as this admiration was provided so readily and frequently in youth. And if while growing up the child somewhat realized the illusion of it, even when it became skeptically received, it was yet at the same time craved. This phenomenon is commonly occurring in love relations, where one likes to hear "the words", hyperbolical and excessive, but still pleasant to the ear and the mind. If the phenomenon is understandable, its excess is problematic. And strangely enough, the more someone has a hard time believing he can be loved, the more he needs to be praised, while at the same time he becomes very suspicious about these praises, and even angry at them. In a preconscious way the addiction and its fictitiousness are somewhat perceived. As well, the imposter recognizes more or less consciously the power one can take over him by granting this craved recognition. He is skeptical of the recognition itself, but also suspicious of the power the praiser takes as someone who grants him recognition: he fears manipulation, he suspects dark intentions. A bit of recognition leaves the imposter wanting more, it awakens the addiction. And the praiser is the "dealer", the one who has the power, since he decides how, when, and how much of the recognition is provided. The praiser, offering recognition, necessarily is also the one who withholds recognition, and he can be hated for it, especially in a love relation. Therefore, we should not be surprised at the endless and powerful dimension of begging and expectations manifested by the individual endowed with a feeling of imposture. Although one main characteristic of the victim of such a scheme, the way he can easily be recognized, is through his susceptibility, his sensitivity, his capacity to easily get angry in an unexpected way. This is understandable, since any phenomenon of addiction implies pain. Pain of the need, pain of anxiety, pain of withdrawal, etc. This strong capacity of irritation, this lack of mental stability, this lack of joy and generosity will be a good indicator that allows us to distinguish the confident person from the arrogant person.

There is another addictive dimension to circumstances, which explains why we allow ourselves to be so determined by them: the filling up of life, a desire for existential saturation. Among the different classical human fears, like fear of heights or fear of loneliness, a common one is the fear of void. In the void, we cannot cling to anything, we have no distraction, nothing can protect us, we are brought face to face with ourselves, constrained to a very intimate vis-à-vis that most likely would make us quite ill at ease. Such an encounter would induce a deep sense of vertigo, since such a mise en abyme is bottomless, endless, like the peeling of an onion: the horizon is pure emptiness, a "more of the same" that leads to a radical absence. Such a metaphysical experience is quite painful, especially if we have always been avoiding it and are not ready for it. But our transcendent being has needs as well, it necessarily forces its self-expression, its surfacing through layers of resistance. And when the subjects are internally forced to allow this reality to come about, they call it depression, and indeed the phenomenon has taken a pathological dimension therefore they look for a cure. In the meantime, in order to postpone as indefinitely as possible such an encounter, they pay close attention to anything that could occupy them, anything that could give them a sense of worth or meaning, anything that could amuse them or make them drunk or forgetful. But our consciousness cannot be bought at such a cheap price, it knows, even when we decide or prefer not to know. Therefore whatever happens, whatever is heard, whatever encounters we have, will more or less activate this consciousness, will either arouse it or dull it, the last option being of course preferable for our empirical self.

The absence of challenge to our being we call "peace", but the real name for such a state is actually "comfort". We can comfortably sit in a cushy armchair and feel at ease, until someone shakes it up or the floor crumbles. But this comfort is very superficial: we are not ready for "anything", we are not prepared for "nothing", we feel at peace within a very determined environment, within specific circumstances. That is the illusion many people entertain, when they need determined situations in order to be peaceful, since they cannot be peaceful in their general life. From which comes the addiction to circumstances, the need for a "safe" environment. This context is generally marked out with obligations and distractions, work, duty, and pleasurable moments. That is why they often have recourse to the idea of "relaxing", since their life is tense, anxious, so they frequently need some panacea to soothe this agitation and edginess. Drinking, socializing, parties, hobbies, meditation, sports, yoga, etc. And it is true that those activities procure some type of relief, in various degrees, but it always remains superficial, since this "relaxing" is bound to circumstances. A relaxation that is in fact substantially impossible. In a way, in this system, there is a rejection of the self. True peace, life tranquility, is considered a boring state, nothingness is a worrisome mirror.

This common form of CI is called by Nietzsche the "religion of comfortableness". In such a scheme, we refuse any inconvenience, annoyance or suffering. The enemy is called "stress", and therefore we want to "relax", without realizing that this relaxing is just a momentary and illusory escape from the problem: the pain caused by our difficulty to challenge ourselves, which naturally is stressful. Instead of taking the bull by the horns, willing and accepting the challenge, we try to escape. In order to establish peace in oneself one should reject comfort, one should take up challenges. One should be authentic rather than greedy. In order to do this, one has to broaden his horizon rather than remaining in his little swamp, warm and cozy. For Bergson, the true personality is a permanent tension, creator of change. It develops at every moment, remaining unpredictable and free. In this sense, it is a dynamic of choice and abandonment, in order to escape the indecision of the promise. He explains that this personality is "littered with the debris of beginnings of being." From such a perspective, we see how the common idea of comfort can only restrain or extinguish the flame of existence.

We can often observe such comfortable behavior. An artificial world of well behaved and boring people that consciously fulfill their obligations, with an occasional non-excessive breach, who need a little drink every evening, who reverentially brush their teeth, who respect dinner ceremony, who have family values, who chat pleasantly, who behave prudently and moderately, who worry about relaxing, who calculate well, who wait for weekends, holidays and special events or rituals in order to enjoy themselves, who wish "have a nice day" to each other or "have a great time". Their life ends, and they could wonder what this was all about. But they have dutifully accomplished their existential "job", they are "nice people". And in their comfort they feel they have reached some ideal. This way of life is even conceptualized in diverse countries, like the "danske hygge": danish wellbeing, or the dutch "gezelligheid", a comfy and cordial setting, some basic and bourgeois hedonist scheme. Any pain, inconvenience or problem is viewed as an enemy, anyone who does not benefit from such bliss engenders pity. Nietzsche claims that such people, contrary to their expectations, ignore happiness, for "happiness and unhappiness are sisters and even twins that either grow up together or, as in your case, remain small together."

Periodic rituals, such as new year celebrations or birthdays formally create a new situation, a new timeline, the semblance of a needed existential transformation. One can artificially create a renewal, tell himself that now he is different. Thus he needs to grant importance to any such event, and the others will comply with such a superficial occurrence. We are far from the ancient idea of ritual as a moment of challenge and growth, even if it was the simple idea of fasting. Rituals are primarily an occasion to feel special for no substantial reason and to consume more than the ordinary, satisfying our gluttony. A moment to compensate artificially with our existential dissatisfaction and monotony, without any substantial existential discontinuity. On this special day, I can reaffirm the greatness and uniqueness of my existence, an irrepressible need that confirms the banality and meaninglessness of my life. Shame to the one that would forget to honor me on that very day.

Another aspect of this addiction is to view life as a series of obligations, which strangely enough are part of the comfort scheme, since it establishes an endless little routine, although an unpleasant one. Commonly, daily activities, the many obligations filling up existence, are viewed as a "job", more than a "work". A "job" is a strenuous or boring activity for which you receive regular payment, or some type or reward. The reward is external to the activity itself, in this sense there is an idea of voluntary bondage or slavery, what Marx calls alienation. It comes out of a primitive need, and not out of an internal spiritual necessity. It is largely connected to obligation, an absence of freedom and choice. There is no accomplishment of the self, unlike in a "work", to the extent we wish to distinguish both terms. Work is this sense both upon the world and upon the self, it then represents its own reward. It constitutes its own end and accomplishment. But indeed, many people view in a way their existence as a "job" rather than a "work".

Chapter 4

Ontological imposture

There is a necessity for psychological expansion in human beings. People want to belong to something larger, bigger, above and beyond the immediate self. From which there is the attraction of the religious experience. We take "religion"in its original sense of "binding", as what connects us. Connecting can have a metaphysical or transcendent sense, bonding us to a higher order of things, a loftier power, a principle of unity, or in a human and immanent sense, bonding us to our brethren and to the empirical world. But in both cases we enlarge our perspective, our world and our identity. In fact the religious phenomenon, throughout history and cultures, generally conflated both functions: relating to transcendence, spiritual, and relating to a community, more worldly. Although one or the other functions can be stronger or weaker, depending on the religion, the culture and the individual. Some persons will practice meditation or engage in esoteric practices, some will become followers of a sports team or a famous star, some will be fascinated by science or literature, but all these apparently diverse activities or engagements have in common that which is beyond his simple self, what has always mesmerized humans.

One could object that the perspective of such an enlargement or ideal does not necessarily imply a sense of imposture. We think it does because we cannot pursue an ideal without thinking that we represent this ideal, that we incarnate it, therefore we internalize it, we make it ours, it provides us with both incentive and legitimacy for our actions. But periodically, we will reflect on our behavior and our undertakings, and we will necessarily realize their limits and even pettiness in relation to the infinity and perfection of the ideal. In those moments, we can never be quite satisfied with our performance. Thus we will oscillate between "manic" moments when we are caught up in the conduct of the activity, in a rather self-righteous and confident attitude, and the "depressive" moments when we envisage the immensity of what should still be done in order to fully accomplish our mission, if that is ever possible. This discrepancy is constitutive of reality, and is an existential necessity, the need of transcendence, but it brings with itself this sense of imposture.

The ontological imposture is a more fundamental scheme, a basic human experience, that one must identify and accept, otherwise it can as well turn into a more painful and pathological pattern. It can be defined as the latent feeling, periodically conscious, of every human being, perceiving his life as meaningless, boring, vain or illusory, but who nevertheless forces himself to play the game of everyday life by pretending to believe in it. Let us explain. It is connected to the principle of nothingness, rather inevitable and constitutive of our own humanity, an anthropological invariant. Man has access to reason, which allows him to think the infinite, a power which makes him attempt to access this infinite, a form or another of the absolute, be it the Cosmos, God, Humanity, Truth, Justice or else. But this infinite is always twofold and dialectical. Nothingness, the negative absolute, as the opposite of the positive absolute, its counterpart, its mirror image, is therefore inevitable and necessary. Opposites are born together, as we know from most religions and philosophies. Any phenomenon naturally generates its opposite by the principle of enantiodromia. Therefore, our mind is naturally oscillating between those two extremes to which we are attracted: they establish the axis on which we think all things, within which we naturally place ourselves. Our identity therefore hangs in the void within this huge ontological gap, somewhat vertiginous. Unconsciously, we place and constitute ourselves within this metaphysical or psychological map. And even though we are caught up in the daily chores of our little empirical life, we cannot help looking up or looking down, with a mixed feeling of fear and joy, anguish and ecstasy. Religious schemes are explicit representations of such a pattern, they generally produce a narrative that makes this ontological principle understandable and usable to guide one's life, where we can feel integrated and legitimized, for example through the principle of an origin of the world or the idea of an ulterior life. Although, with the abandonment of religion, the individual becoming its own finality and reality, as Kant described it, this fundamental framework is somewhat lost and can easily produce a pathological effect, unless it finds another way to become conscious and meaningful, for example through philosophical thinking. Nevertheless, a purely psychological explanation of the phenomenon seems to us quite inadequate to deal with this issue, although it can somewhat help to tone down the anxiety: there are metaphysical issues, the necessity of dealing with the transcendent dimension of the self. This implies to deal with the general problems of human finitude, as each and every one of us inevitably and personally experiences it. But most individuals try to ignore this crucial issue by remaining focused on their immediate empirical preoccupations, what we call survival mentality, although this principle can more or less generally function, with its ups and downs.

These metaphysical considerations are paradoxical. On one hand, the mind looks at the positive absolute, with its power and beauty, it is attracted by some form of perfection, if it wants, it can admire it and benefit from this contemplation. On the other side we can regret our incapacity to reach such sublime reality, our difficulty to grant it some reality in our own existence. The consciousness of our personal mortality, with the concept of immortality in the background, is the most obvious manifestation of this tension. We therefore look down on ourselves as a miserable creature, a sinner, a sad mortal, a weak and vulnerable being. Our glance is inevitably attracted to the negative absolute, to which we are just as much attracted, which often seems even closer to us, more reachable than the positive absolute. It is easier and more natural for us to think we are nothing or nothingness rather than thinking we are God. The latter perspective is possible and tempting, but it is hard to maintain, since the reality principle always pursues us with its harsh reminders. And when we look at the infinite universe, at the immensity of knowledge, at the endlessness of human struggles, at our daily difficulties with life, it is hard to conserve a feeling of greatness: we cannot avoid realizing how limited and meaningless our little being is. Therefore, all our endeavors to exist in this infinite background, our desire to believe in ourself and our own significance, can easily appear as illusory and fraudulent, as a mere shadow, in spite of all our efforts to "make it", or to "fake it". Although the distinction between illusion and reality, between pretending and being is not always clear cut, as the expression "Fake it until you make it"indicates, a principle which definitely bears some reality.

How can we not periodically think that this busy life we lead is nothing more than a Sisyphean task, permanently rolling up a stone that will eternally fall, existence being a mere punishment. We are as meaningless as those ants we observe, going back and forth in tight columns, carrying some measly bread crumbs to some unknown destination, which someone could destroy with a simple foot stomp or a mere spray of insecticide. But we pursue our endeavors, trying to avoid those depressing thoughts, although they are tenacious and remain in the background of our minds, eternally witnessing our pretense and deceit while we proceed in our daily routines. What will be left when we die? A terrible question we prefer to avoid, although it cannot be avoided. At least, if we faced it, we could reconcile ourselves with our own finitude, but since we prefer to conceal this reality, we know in the bottom of our hearts that we are impostors, a healthy reminder of this undesirable reality.

For example, a true Christian always feels like an impostor: he preaches faith in the good when he knows he is a sinner. Since he never really fully does what he preaches, he remains conscious of his own shortcomings. Paradoxically, if he does not feel like an impostor, then he is really an impostor: he is basking in his feeling of good conscience, being sincere about his own goodness, without any authenticity. After all, how can he deny the reality of the original sin, the historical loss of a first and mythical paradise, an alienation constitutive of one's own humanity. We could at this point insert a conceptual difference between faith and belief: the first knows the anguish of doubt, the second is self-satisfied. And this phenomenon is true for any scheme endowed with a moral ideal. Therefore, to reconcile with our own shortcomings is to reconcile with our own self, allowing man to be a "bridge", as Nietzsche coined it, instead of being focused on defending and protecting some fictitious existential production, the main source of our pains and misery.

For Hegel, self-consciousness is the highest level the mind can and should reach, on its way to the absolute. And he views two components to such a realization.

On one side, there should be an action upon the world, a challenging task accomplished on the outside. The individual will exercise his power by transforming his environment, transforming himself by the same token. And of course, such a task is accomplished with the idea of a purpose, with a goal that incarnates an ideal, although never fully achieved. A lack from which derives the feeling of imposture, since one is ever at the height of his intention, he always comes short of necessity. So it is for these brilliant characters, entrepreneur, artist, political leader or other, who know how to act on an external "matter", often in an excessive way although creative. Totally turned towards their work, obsessed by it, moved by an unbridled passion or an implacable will, they ignore tranquility or moderation, they are anxious, easily angry or aggressive, their relationships with others are difficult or absent. They are centered on a power of being that they hardly know how to contain, the slightest impediment bothers them. They are permanently threatened by their own unaccomplishment. When they speak about "their" goals, they are often too vague or too concrete. They are mainly the result of comparisons to others, to those around them, if not the result of social pressure. "My" goals are not actually "mine". Therefore, the feeling of existential failure arises from two main elements: the will to immediately satisfy superficial desires and the comparison with others, if not their injunction.

On the other side, there should be a work on oneself, in the form of some introspection. It implies a "care of the self", as Foucault specified it, inspired by philosophers of Greek antiquity. It is both to know oneself and to work on the self, challenging oneself and daring to contemplate one's limits and needs for improvement. There again, there is a perspective of ideal that is never fully attained, facing once more the sense of imposture. This sense of ideal should affect both our actions and our personal life. In a way, our little person becomes secondary in relation to this ideal. The individual is not an end in itself, but a mere means for something much larger than himself. Thus in spite of all his endeavors, he cannot not see himself as a miserable creature, but in a detached way. He accepts that in spite of his measly efforts to improve the world and become himself better, there is something derisory and pathetic in his being and his attempts, a terrible feeling compensated by the identification to this ideal. He pretends to represent something which is so far from him, but he consoles himself since he somewhat partakes of it.

Thus there are two forms of critical thinking, two competencies that bear the same name but are actually different, since a subject can be competent in one but not in the other, for psychological and cognitive reasons. They can be distinguished as critical thinking toward oneself and critical thinking toward the outside. The first one implies awareness of the subject, the thinking, feeling and perceiving subject, who becomes an object for himself. The second one implies awareness of the object, of everything that is not the subject, although it can easily imply ignoring subjects in general. For example, the psychologist is rather interested in the subject, normally including himself, when the scientist is more interested in the nature and understanding of the world. It is the common distinction we encounter in 19th century German philosophy, between the geisteswissenschaft, science of the mind or humanities, and the naturwissenschaft, science of nature or physical sciences. For Hegel, as for Goethe and Schiller, the ideal is to combine both of them in a sort of dialectical relation, since they are in some way indissociable. And to separate them represents a sort of epistemological failure, and we could say it constitutes an imposture, through a truncated vision of reality. As we already find it in Plato, inspired by the Delphi maxim: "Know thyself, you will know the gods and the universe". Indeed, to pretend knowing the world without knowing the instrument through which we know the world, or knowing ourselves without confronting ourself to the world, seems rather self-delusory.

Lastly, any value that drives us is in principle an abstract concept. Therefore, it justifies itself, it is unconditional, otherwise it is only the manifestation of another more substantial or fundamental value. This concept is not a construction, its elaboration is not rational, it is not the product of a reasoning. It usually refers to a personal experience, something that touches us closely without knowing its reason. It is therefore not an entity, except by a derivative meaning that we attribute to it, hypostatizing this experience. So it is with reason, God, Dao, justice, beauty, etc. These concepts only have reality through a feeling, a drive, a vision, a passion, etc., otherwise they are just words, hollow formalisms.

Often the individual is not aware of this value that drives him. But he will easily use the term "improvement", for example in the education of children or in his own life, under various meanings that remain vague, a mixture of cognitive, psychological, moral, physical, etc. But it must be remembered that the concept of "improvement" implies a presupposition of "better". And if there is a "better", then there is a "good", and therefore a specific value which will embody this "good". Be it reason, truth, justice, peace, health, strength or whatever. Of course, we are often oblivious to this, so we are content with a vague concept of "improvement". But embedded in "improvement" necessarily hides a transcendent finality, an absolute, even if not declared. And curiously, "improvement", despite the satisfaction it provides, is never truly satisfactory, since there is always a lack, a sort of Sisyphean dimension of being.

Chapter 5

The two impostures (Ontological impostor: OI, Circumstantial impostor: CI)

The OI derives his internal authority from himself, he is accountable only to himself and to his ideal. This does not imply negating or avoiding the principle of reality, conveyed by the objectivity of his results and the feedback or criticism coming from other people. But he will not be determined by them, he will not permanently hope or request confirmation, compliments or praise, he will not be obsessed with the immediacy of results, since he is conscious of the ambition of his ideal. He is attached to his enterprise, and even though results and approbation are obviously welcome, he never loses track of his ideal, a never ending and immense venture. In opposition the CI clings to results and praise, his mental state is determined by them, his ideals are precisely those results and praise and he always fears being exposed as a fraud, while the OI remains aloof and equanimous in his quest.

One significant difference between the OI and the CI is on the emotional level: the former tends to be sad when the latter tends to be angry. The reason for this is that OI thinks the problem relies on his own inner being, on his "nature", which he can regret or lament but he knows that fundamentally it will not and cannot be changed, therefore he is sad. The CI is very much outer oriented, he is more heteronomous, and he views the outside, other persons and circumstances, as the main cause of his misery. He is unhappy with them, he thinks they should be different, or act differently, but since he does not know how to deal with it, he feels impotent and victimized, he gets angry or resentful. The CI is as well an OI, since it is an anthropological invariant, but he chooses to focus on outside causes to account for his own problems. They are easier and more comfortable explanations, although such options create numerous problems in his existence. The world is unfair, people are bad, we do not get what we deserve are the most commonplace clichés. Thus the CI remains very sensitive to contextual parameters, he will pick up and dramatize any event that he will consider threatening or unpleasant to his wishful identity, he will hyperbolize anything seeming to deprive him of his legitimate needs.

The OI as well can be sensitive to external events, but when some unfortunate episode occurs, he will invariably focus on his own being and conclude that he is the main source of the problem, or being fatalist, he accepts the wretched nature of the world. Thus, he suppresses his expectations, he folds in upon himself, a withdrawal which leads to a feeling of sadness or depression. Any vexatious incident just echoes in him his own worthlessness. Since the CI views his problems as other people's fault, he wishes to eliminate the unwanted situation, presupposing that after such an elimination everything will be fine. But since it is often out of his control, he feels powerless and becomes angry. An important point is that he cannot accept his share of responsibility on these issues, as that would be too painful for him, a denial that makes him even more powerless and resentful.

For the OI, being bad, inadequate or worthless is an internal feature of reality, it comes together with our "being oneself", this feature tends to relate to our individual nature, even define it. Thus, the state of things appears unchangeable, from which easily derives a sense of despair, sadness or hopelessness, feelings which are of a rather passive nature, in spite of their potential intensity. Ontological imposture describes an actuality, the harsh internal discrepancy and fracture of our own self, hardly anything can be done about it, it has no beginning and no end, it is "just"the way it is. The world vision is different for the circumstantial imposture, since the "badness", discrepancy or insufficiency is connected to the environment, to an external cause. For right or wrong, what is external is considered negotiable or changeable, therefore it can be eliminated through some action, with some force: the world should be adjustable at will. Any defect should be corrected to satisfy the subject, otherwise he will express his wrath, a powerless attempt to manifest his power. Although constantly faced with the ineffectiveness of his anger, the CI will channel his dissatisfaction into a permanent state of resentment, hiding his pain in a passive aggressive behavior, with periodical open expressions of his outrage.

A crucial element that sets apart the nature of both worldviews is that unlike in the case of "being", circumstances have a beginning and an end, those phenomena have identifiable causes which can therefore be altered or halted. Reality is viewed as accidental, not as essential. This can explain as well why sadness is for the OI a more lingering background feeling: it is less subjected to particular events, it is in a way more "self-generated", thus more ontological. One can feel sad as a general state of the soul, as a way of being, without the need of a particular troubling event. Anger is an active emotion that appears primarily as a reaction to an event. Anger cannot sustain itself for long, so it is by definition circumstantial, both because of its nature and its cause. Of course, momentary anger can channel itself in a permanent "cold" state, in the form of resentment. But there again resentment, the expression of victimhood, is most likely connected to external conditions, nourished by some permanent circumstances. For example, we often get excited or depressed by the place we occupy, by the surroundings, but with a minimal degree of consciousness, little by little, we realize that it is what we do there that matters, and even more what we accomplish there.

Another significant difference between the two schemes is on the issue of consciousness, or more specifically self-consciousness. In this context, self-consciousness, or self-awareness, indicates the presence of the subject to himself, the realization of his nature and of his limits, and the recognition of his subjective interpretation of the world. More radically, the understanding that the world is primarily defined as a projection of one's own vision.

While consciousness is being aware of one's environment and body and lifestyle, self- consciousness is the recognition of that awareness. Self-consciousness is how an individual consciously knows and understands his own character, feelings, motives, and desires, and identifies how their subjective nature determines his apprehension of the world. Of course, this philosophical sense should not be confused with the common meaning of the term, rather the opposite, which indicates an acute worry about what other people think about him, judging his appearance and actions, accompanied by a nervous and uncomfortable sensation. Philosophical self-consciousness, with a capacity to take distance from oneself and exercise a self-critical ability, represents a heightened form of relation to reality.

Freud proposed an interesting concept "unheimlich", which literally means "unhomey", strange and not comfortable, a disturbing strangeness, which is also used to refer to something unconcealed, what has been revealed, generally against one's will: the exposure of our intimacy. Schelling wrote that "Unheimlich is the name for everything that ought to have remained secret and hidden but has come to light". The term is connected to the "slip of the tongue", when the subconscious momentarily shows itself and a subject can himself be surprised of what he hears. According to Freud we are the most uncanny thing for ourselves. This explains the general unwillingness to look in the depths of one's soul or mind, for fear of discovering something unwanted. So, we are unheimlich for ourselves, not at home in our own being, having something foreign living in us. Dependent on a degree of one's self-acceptance, this unhomeyness will either be fought against or simply contemplated. In the former case the sense of fracture will be denied, one will want to pretend in order to maintain the illusion of a wholesome self, the CI scheme, and in the latter case the eeriness of oneself does not disappear, but is observed peacefully or not, the OI scheme.

Thus, the OI, by focusing on his own worldview and its discrepancy with some form of absolute, is more capable of reason, more inclined towards a deeper analysis of things. He is more available to reality as what escapes his personal power of understanding, as a permanent challenge to his own thinking. While the CI, since he reacts immediately and in a negative way to the surrounding world, entertains a more reduced horizon, does not question his own perspective, and maintains a strong bias toward otherness. He reacts positively or negatively to external solicitations and interactions: things are good when they please him and coax him, bad when they irritate him or fail to comply with his expectations. He is not so concerned about understanding and being challenged, he remains in a very subjective scheme. He will instinctively twist his interpretation of events and people as it fits his pre-established subjective scheme. Of course, he entertains a rather painful relation to reality, since he operates in a survival mode: he always feels threatened by what might happen, he has too much to lose.

The CI easily gets scandalized, for he erected his behavior in a moral scheme, where of course he is the victim and the "good person", when the others tend to be immoral, careless, thoughtless and inconsiderate. In comparison, the OI is more accepting, since the imperfections he encounters just recall his own flaws and deficiencies. Although we can identify a potential drawback as well in the OI: he devalues so much his own identity that he is obsessed by his own imperfection, an extreme case that can make him impotent and depressed, in a way an extreme form of narcissism, since he focuses primarily on himself, in a self-destructive way. But he then has lost the appropriate ontological perspective.

In daily life, we often use dramatic expressions to qualify or describe what happens to us, to account for the effect of circumstances. Of course, we should not deny that some events can be particularly painful, physically or morally. But we will notice that those expressions are often abusive, although interesting and revealing. For example the word "disaster", which etymologically indicates that we have "lost the stars", those stars that guide us, that allow us to find our place and our way in the cosmos. Or "devastated", which means that our being is "laid waste", annihilated, reduced to nothing, because of the terrible damage accomplished, forgetting that our being transcends most of what we consider as the phenomenon of devastation. Actually, the disaster or the devastation is accomplished way before what we consider devastating or disastrous. The circumstances just reveal a previous phenomenon, of ontological nature, that we were not conscious of. The referred event just sets the scene and renders visible our true, antecedent and more profound existential drama. Thus, without an ideal, without an unconditional perspective, we are condemned to anxiety, to drama, to anger, to resentment.

The CI, tormented and weakened by his feeling of insecurity, his anxiety about himself and the world, has strong needs. Need to possess, need to control, need to exist, need to assert and prove himself, need for status, need to compete, he is engaged in a permanent race for his survival. Therefore, he has opinions, he has to justify and defend them, he has to claim ownership for what emanates from his mouth, he is addicted to copyright and does not want "his"ideas to be "stolen", he has to take stands on everything, to agree or disagree, he has to show that he is different and special, he claims to be an independent person, he must stand out since he fears being banal and disappearing into a dark ocean of undifferentiation, engulfed in the mass. The OI, more fatalist about the order of things, is not so bothered by those issues, he is not engaged in a quest for recognition, he is more worried about his own being as the main existential issue. For him, the spirit blows where it wants, when it wants, how it wants; he lets publishers worry about copyright. Diverse problems encountered on the way will rather be taken peacefully as a challenge or an opportunity to exist in a substantial way. The true battle is with himself, not with the world, although the world is both the witness and the battleground for his own struggle. The CI is easily scandalized, he has strong moral demands from others, while the OI is focused on exerting power upon himself, he works on accepting himself, as a condition for facing reality.

For those reasons, the CI is rather a noluntarist: he easily criticizes, both to prove his specificity and to express his dissatisfaction with the world. He has a compulsive tendency to find flaws everywhere, from which his competitive attitude comes. He will go out of his way to put down what other people do, others hardly find favor in his eyes: he is neither understanding, nor generous, nor patient. He will often know what he does not want but not be so clear with what he does want. More than anything, he does not want to expose the poverty and the nakedness of his little being. The noluntarist, the naysayer, is choleric and aggressive. His compelling desire for representing perfection, moral, cognitive or else, inhibits his capacity for decision and action: he tends to complicate things and to procrastinate, pretending to be exhaustive and rigorous. He can be pedantic or pompous, he aspires to the "never done", he claims the unprecedented. Or he will be very impulsive, but not substantially thoughtful. He gets bogged down in a trap: the lie of the enormous, the illusion of the grandiose and the impossible. He has no clue about what he wants, he could not name it: it is beyond words or any concrete representation, it is endless and indeterminate. The OI is demanding, first of all with himself, and he can apply or not this same demand to others. But he remains conscious of the difficulty or even the impossibility of his expectations, a consciousness which makes him more understanding, indulgent and patient. He recognizes the smallness of his self, when facing the sublime of the ideal he admires and pursues. Thus he can as well step aside, he can withdraw himself and welcome what is, let things happen by themselves, since he is conscious that the countless phenomena have their own reasons to occur, which he can neither understand nor control.

As an additional remark, let us affirm that strangely enough, the OI, in spite of his anguished nature since he permanently faces his own frailty and infirmity, is more peaceful and joyful than the CI. In substance, beside instances of exaltation or excitement, in the heat of the moment, he does not pretend to be other than what he is, he tends to be more reconciled with reality, mainly the first and most substantial aspect of it: the self. The self, "being" as we intimately and daily experience it. Through this experience, he remains conscious of the order of the world because he does not attempt to deny it, to refuse it, to warp it or to forget it. Thus he notices the potential good residing in this world, no matter how minute it is, since he identifies to some positive principle illuminating reality, thus mitigating his sadness and providing him with a peaceful joy. The CI is rather engaged in a constant struggle with this self, primarily because he tries to deny its finite reality, refusing the unbearable face to face encounter with himself. And naturally, the pain caused by this impossible struggle turns its glance toward the outside as a quest for relief. But the outside, being the outside, unpredictable and out of control, never up to the level of his expectations, constantly provides reasons to be disappointed, frustrated, angry and resentful. His world is disenchanted, scanty light is shed on it, it is somber and squalid.

The CI often maintains of course a negative worldview. The basic scheme is "The world is bad or ugly, I am bad or ugly". This negative dimension of the world, deprived of any possibility of salvation since nothing transcends it, will necessarily engender problems. Numerous are the causes that can be instinctively invoked by the subject in order to explain his own negative features or actions. And when he attempts to justify himself, he does it through blaming the world, through an externalization of the badness. His problems are due to his education, to his family, to his society, to his handicap, to his environment, all these judgments irremediably condemning the sad nature of things or the ugly reality. Even the concept of "bad luck", often used by some persons, tells us how the world is badly made, since not only the causality principle ensures things are bad, but mere random events manage to produce negative consequences. We could oppose such a vision for example the concept of serendipity, the French expression "hazard does things well", or the idea of providence. Therefore, he ends up always being a victim, since this allows him to externalize anything bad and not be responsible for it, a rationale that can explain his resentment. If the OI is fully responsible for his own existence, its accomplishments and shortcomings, the CI attributes much of his existence to the outside .In a way, he negates himself, abandons his freedom; he will naturally complain, even claiming without realizing it that his identity was stolen.

One interesting feature of the CI is the "private"relation he sometimes maintains to his own "badness". He will for example claim openly that he is bad, he wants to be heard, but he denies to anyone else the right to say the same thing. He is the only one who has the right to such a claim, he refuses to others the possibility of such negative judgments. Worse, he is rather expecting compliments, he is addicted to them. Thus, one can wonder why he makes such disparaging declarations about himself if he does not want anyone else to do the same. It seems that those comments about himself are used as a tool for self-protection, as a shield, like when someone presents his work and starts by saying "it is not so good", "it is only a first draft", "I am not so happy with this work", etc. One simple explanation is that by saying those words, he will exorcize any potential criticism, hoping that in return the listener will "console"him, will offer him compliments, by saying "not at all, it's very good", or at least "it's not so bad, there are some good points". He thus tries to keep control of the general assessment of his work. Furthermore he practices a sort of emotional blackmail, since after this avowal of "badness", no one will dare add anything in this direction so as not to add to the load. Another strategy is to make derogatory statements about oneself in an ironical way, for example:

"that's me, always dumb", where obviously the speaker thinks he is smart by saying this, and he would get upset if anyone else called him dumb.

The ontological impostor views himself as lowly, in relation to the clear ideal he admires or pursues; he realizes he is far from it. Either he does not suffer from it, accepting this situation as a feature of reality, or he suffers from it but is not resentful about it, he accepts this suffering, viewing it as a constitutive part of his own reality. The OI can entertain either a tragic or peaceful vision of his discrepancy with the ideal. Most times, he does not merely contemplate in an impotent fashion this discrepancy, he works on it, he tries to improve himself, in spite of the fact he knows he will never, far from it, reach his ideal. Some classical examples are the Christian scheme, with its godly perspective; the Stoics, who thought that to live a good life, one has to understand and apply the rules of the natural order; or the communists, who sacrifice their personal existence in order to satisfy the common good. But when we examine numerous traditional legends in many cultures, we can notice that they describe the discrepancy between a subject and some ideal, and how obstacles have to be overcome in order to satisfy this ideal.

When there is a drama, when some event is painful or troublesome, naturally, the mind seeks for some form of psychological or existential relief. It needs a "fall back" option. And this option becomes the background on which everything else plays, the paradigmatic pivot; it surges and establishes itself as a matrix of meaning, as a grounding for any sense, even as a causal principle. As the axis of reliance, as the ultimate altar of repose, no matter how shaky or elusive it is, it takes a hold on us, it invades us, it inhabits us and lives in us. Without it, we are too affected by every sad event happening in our life, as we are isolated, a mere separated, particular and meaningless being.

For the CI, this backdrop, framework or scene is otherness: the others or the other, some unique evildoer, or a setting, a context, in any case some identifiable cause of our difficulty, some specific agent of our doldrum. This way, he can externalize his pain, transfer his ill being to the outside, focus it on an alien source, in an attempt to exorcize his discomfort or torment, in order to expel it, to relieve it, to diminish it. He therefore needs some definite enemy, a scarecrow against which he can concentrate his anger or resentment, thus he fabricates for himself a useful, reassuring and releasing foe. As the mean gods from another epoch, this powerful, vicious and deleterious force, by providing some form of explanation for our misery, allows us to reintegrate this rupture of harmony in a globally coherent scheme. Of course, if this type of phenomenon occurs too frequently, it is our whole world vision which now feels threatened. That is the "disaster", literally meaning "losing the stars", when our personal cosmos is shattered, torn to pieces, reality becoming meaningless, distressing and unendurable. But at least we have a scapegoat to curse and to hate, in a sort of permanent demonic ritual which at least provides us with some existential meaning. Short of this fallback option, we can only face the unbearable face of the abyss, the gloomy vertigo of nothingness.

For the OI, this backdrop, framework or scene is as well otherness, but in a different sense. First of all it is not a concrete and immediate otherness, but a more radical one, in the "rooting" sense, rather abstract and transcendent. As well, this otherness does not have a negative but a positive sense, since it is an ideal we admire or attempt to reach, and not a dangerous and threatening entity. Then it is constitutive of the self and fulfilling rather than painful. As well, it points toward some activity and accomplishment rather than making us an impotent and suffering victim. There is still a form of agony, since we envisage the impossibility of this ideal, but it takes the form and feeling of the sublime, as we described it earlier. We suffer from not reaching it, but its contemplation makes us joyful and peaceful because of its dimension of eternity, its nature of absolute in which we participate, that in a way belongs to us since we identify to it. Its beauty and power echoes in our being, protecting us from being too affected by the sad events affecting our empirical existence, stopping us from being overwhelmed by torment and drama. It therefore provides us with a certain cognitive and emotional stability and does not make us feel impotent. We can maintain ourselves beyond ourselves, since caring about our self is the opposite of caring about our person. We experience the presence of an unconditional and primordial reality. Instead of feeling scattered and discombobulated, this ideal makes us merge with a form of unity, by identifying with something much larger than ourself, thus providing tranquility to our soul. The call of being is too deafening, one has to dull his ear in order to soften the sound or to totally silence it.

The feeling of meaninglessness is a natural occasional state of all individuals, CI or OI just as well, and since an individual is never a pure spirit or merely a radical idealist, one can oscillate between ontological consolation, contemplating the ideal and acting in this perspective, more demanding, and circumstantial consolation, with easy satisfactions. The opposition between superficial and ephemeral reliefs by merely changing something about the circumstances, by pleasing oneself, and self-challenge, plays as well on the differences of level in self-consciousness. Thus we might oscillate between OI and CI compensations, and one might indeed easily confuse the techniques to self-console, especially if we are a bit desperate. Cramming down food or drink, sexual activity, browbeating a partner or other persons, going to the gym, buying goods... It's cheap, but it works as a panacea to hide the pain for a moment. One temporarily feels relief. But It results in greater depression because it can only be pretend to console. Therefore we will permanently hesitate between a primitive care of the self, where we satisfy primitive needs and desires, and a higher level care of the self, where we engage in a more profound activity, challenging ourselves and sell-accomplishing. But the latter practice needs a minimum of distance, self-consciousness and mental energy in order to be set in motion.

As we have already outlined it, the ontological imposture and the circumstantial imposture do not stand out from each other in a clear and distinct way, it seems to us that there is a kind of permanent oscillation around which the existential stakes are articulated. An interesting case of this phenomenon is the story of Cinderella. She has the status of a poor servant, despised and ignored by her environment. She was beautiful and kind, but her value was not recognized. As a result, despite her proven qualities, she doubted her own merit, while at the same time she cried over her miserable fate, because "she would like to...", she was always animated by a certain hope. She longs for something else, she feels within herself the feeling of another life, another status, another meaning, something more valuable and more wonderful. However, thanks to an unexpected providence, a powerful godmother and then a charming prince, she can still realize her dream, which nevertheless remains fragile, conditioned by time and circumstances. She will finally be recognized, but will not hold any grudges from her unhappy past, quite the contrary. We can conclude from this story that on the one hand Cinderella is determined by circumstances, which affect and determine her, since depending on the case she will be happy or unhappy: she needs external recognition. But on the other hand, she transcends these circumstances, since her kindness and generosity remain constant, they are not affected by the circumstances. We find in this character this tension or oscillation of existence, between the less than nothing of the servant and the marvelousness of the princess. Servant, she dreams of being a princess, princess, she remembers her status as a servant since she continues to help her "naughty" sisters, however repentant. This existential mise en abyme, where the two extremes of a fractured identity remain face-to-face and in tension, nevertheless tends to expose us to an ontological imposture, despite the circumstantial determinations that constitute the narration.

Circumstantial thinking is not plastic, it cannot not go through a paradigm shift, because it would have to abandon its posture, even momentarily, a rather painful perspective, since the circumstance is viewed as its framework, as the condition of its satisfaction or identity. One needs to have access to some meta level in order to accept such a shifting. In this sense, the ontological view is a pivot, the axis around which rotate the circumstances, the "stance" of the "circum", and the circumstances thus remain contingent. The OT can fight against these circumstances. But this "ontological rebel" is conscious of the nature of the circumstances and of their limits, he can decide to ignore them, or he can fight with them, but he never becomes obsessed with them, as he does not erect them as a necessity or an absolute. The circumstantial thinker either abides painfully by the circumstances, or he desperately fights against them, but he does not entertain any perspective beyond it: the circumstances define the limits of his own world, in a positive or negative way. He therefore is caught in a given paradigm that cannot be problematized. The ontological thinker can simultaneously commit himself and be detached, in a paradoxical way, when the circumstantial thinker either fights or abandons. in a logical way. As a consequence, the CT claims the right to his opinions and feelings. But since the OT maintains a relation to some form of transcendence, he views those opinions and feelings as some transitory moment to which he does not cling. He perceives what happens to him within the background of an emptiness, a groundlessness, an infinite perspective which keeps in check any glorifications of thoughts and events. The criticism or deconstruction of his thinking system does not bother him, he presupposes it as the lawful outcome of events, just as the seasons endlessly follow each other. The demise of his thinking is banal, he can never become of those zealots who project in their own words a statute, a solid grounding, a determined identity or the inevitable passage of any reflection, an obligatory conceptual framework. The OT has no needs, no obligations, no addiction, no refuge, he acts freely, he permanently keeps a dialectical relation and a tension between his affirmations or engagements and indetermination or chaos. Any harmonious principle or causal determination constantly faces some type of arbitrariness or contingency.

Let us propose the idea that the OT is a person, when the CT is an individual. The term "person", from the latin persona indicates the mask of the actor, which can be removed and changed, when the term "individual", from the Latin "individuus", indicates what cannot be divided, some solid indestructible entity, like the term "atom", from the Greek word "atomos": what cannot be divided or destroyed. The "individual"will therefore try to look for or attempt to establish some "true self", he will cling for this to some predicates of his existence, while the "person"realizes the mobility, the fragility and evanescence of this self, never true nor false, just operational and contingent, always multiple and shifting according to the interaction between his own will and circumstances, internal or external, between possibility and aspirations. Let us remember here of the first philosophical sentences ever written in Greek, by Anaximandre: "Genesis and decline, decline and genesis".

Chapter 6

The false ontological impostor

Following the feedback of some initial readers, we realized there was a phenomenon we had not really considered in our description of the ontological imposture that we need to clarify in order to avoid confusion. We call this phenomenon the false ontological impostor, or the latent circumstantial impostor. A priori, when we listen to these people, they easily tell us how bad they find themselves, how ugly they seem, how meaningless or stupid they are, etc. They are bad, and there is nothing else to it, an acknowledgment that could lead us to conclude to an ontological interpretation, since in the present speech we do not notice any context or external cause: things are what they are, and the subject seems to be conscious of the problem of his self and readily admits it. But, when we hear these people speak, we cannot avoid getting slightly suspicious. Our initial impression is that they are overdoing it, they are putting on a show, overplaying their nothingness. It is always rather strange when someone whips himself publicly and confesses so blatantly his shortcomings, unless it is for a very short moment, out of surprise for example, as a reaction to an unexpected event. So we can wonder about the reasons for such a "confession", and determine why it should not be taken as a real sense of ontological imposture. The main reason is that there is no explicit sense of ideal, or it is too vague, too removed. There is just the idea of being bad, being worthless, but not in a context of a wider perspective. There is just the dullness or insignificance of one's self, nothing beyond it. There is no discrepancy, no perspective, just the bare flatness of a personal reality, which probably rubs off on the world. Because of this, the subject is caught in himself, in his feeling bad, deprived of any real consciousness: he is just himself, that is all there is to it, there is no regulatory ideal. In a way, they become their own circumstance, and they can be assimilated to the CI. Unlike the OI, they do not benefit from any form of ideal or absolute, there is no higher principle: they are the exclusive center of the world. They only see themselves, indulging in a miserable vision of themselves. As a consequence, they either get depressed or they find a derivative that allows them to forget. Another case of false ontological impostor, rather different, is the shy person who often is a hidden megalomaniac. The basic principle of such persons is that they display a humble and fearful attitude, they do not dare express themselves. But when they take the risk of revealing their inner being, we are often surprised at the sudden shift. They are pretentious, they demand and expect a lot, they are disrespectful of others, they think something is owed to them, some type of recognition or status. Actually, their initial silence can be explained by their apprehension about the external judgment: the fear that observers would not perceive how great they are, that they would utter negative judgments about their person. Being quite insecure since they expect a lot, they prefer to remain folded upon themselves, not taking the risk of any criticism or rejection. Let us not forget that the more a subject hopes to obtain some recognition from others, the more he is greedy, the more anxious he will be about being disappointed, a disappointment that in some cases can be intuited as psychologically unbearable. Therefore, this shy person will wait for the moment he deems opportune to unveil himself, either because the circumstances are appropriate, because he is with the right persons, or because he has waited long enough and cannot be patient anymore, he might then explode. And the witnesses of such a "conversion" will be surprised by the violence of the shift. But this shy megalomaniac, even though he does not explain his own behavior in terms of what other people do to him, and seems focused on himself, is definitely not an OI. First of all, because in such a system there is no ideal, the subject is his own center of reality. Second, because the shy person is very preoccupied and determined by the judgments of other persons, even if he does not explicitly admit it, internally to himself and openly to others. "I have been like this since I started working". "I became worried when I had children". "I was not like this when I was younger", says the false OI. They speak as if the other person or a situation had the power to make them become something other than what they were. In general, events in our life bear rather a revealing function, more than a causal function. Difficult or challenging situations make manifest the nature of our being, which otherwise could remain more hidden. Circumstances reveal our relation to others and our relation to an ideal. The only exception we might make to this principle would concern highly traumatic events, which then take on a pathological form.

Chapter 7

Transcendence and divertissement

Any person, no matter how little educated or self-conscious periodically attempts to escape his empirical self and accede to "something else", as a means of relief, of relaxation, of freedom, of joy, of excitement, something that allows breaking out of the routine that constitutes a large proportion of our existence. What we can call transcendence, is exceeding the self or escaping the self. This "something else" that can act as a form of consolation, of diversion, of alleviation of our existential pain, boredom, anxiety. Without forgetting the permanent threat of meaninglessness that distresses and torments the human soul. Pascal calls it "divertissement", which has a sense of entertainment, of recreation, of distraction. To entertain originally indicates an idea of maintaining, of caring, or looking after, which implies that entertainment helps us to attend after our own existence. Recreation originally means to create again, to renew, a renewal of life and mind, and it refers to the fact that one is doing things in order to enjoy himself, in opposition to work or obligation, rather painful. Distraction has both meanings of diversion, of interruption, of breaking away, and of enjoyment, which implies that our usual life is dreary and dull. We can therefore understand the importance of such activities, which strangely enough we can relate to a need for transcendence. Originally, to transcend is "to climb across", from which its actual meaning of going beyond usual limits, to escape normal ways, to get out of the established routine, to surpass oneself, etc. Listening to music, visiting friends, taking a walk in the park, playing a game, having a drink, eating a good meal, dancing, gardening, are many examples of those leisures or hobbies we use in order to go beyond usual life and escape survival obligations. Listening to music, a very popular activity, is a good example of this common transcendance. We stop struggling, we stop competing, we stop worrying, we stop complaining, we abandon ourselves to some form of aesthetic experience, taking us beyond the boundaries of common existence.

Nevertheless, something is missing in these types of experiences. A priori, it lacks the challenging dimension of the self necessary for a substantial access to transcendence, the confrontation to oneself, the "wall of fire" to be crossed, necessary to truly transcend ourselves, what is called "putting skin in the game". There has to be some stakes in such endeavor, the exercise needs some type of peril, primarily the danger of failure, the effort needed to succeed, the difficulty which implies that we become an object of work for ourself, a task where we can contemplate our own limits, where we realize that there is a dimension of impossibility in our pursuit. And this criteria brings us back to the opposition between OI and CI. The OI is conscious of the value he pursues, and conscious of the discrepancy between his empirical self and this value. But in spite of the sadness or anguish this generates in him, he pursues what is missing, consoling himself with the greatness of his task and the fact he partakes in the admired value.

The CI has no clear value, he pursues the desires of his empirical self, always frustrated that his expectations are not fulfilled, be it of possession, recognition, power, being loved or else, to name the most classic pursuits, always in a reduced context. He only gets little compensation here and there, never really satisfying. Or he has more or less managed to organize for himself a tranquil little life, surrounded by persons that will not trouble him, but his equilibrium is rather superficial, it will be easily destabilized by events from the outside, or by an unusual and threatening encounter or dialogue. Too many taboos are encrusted, the balance is fragile. Thus it is obvious that the latter has more needs to escape, more needs for divertissement, and the last thing he needs would be a challenge and the risk of failure. When the OI on the other side, if he does not ignore those little "happinesses", to quote Hannah Arendt, he does not view them as fundamental and substantial, he does not overinvest them, he does not know the depression of the after, the psychological "hangover"of those limited existential compensations, and therefore he does not develop some type of addiction to them. There is "transcendence"and "transcendence", some modality of being more worthy, more substantial and therefore more constructive and rewarding than others. But the inertia that plagues the human soul leads him too often to prefer the option of pettiness. Little men, as Chinese philosophy calls them, in opposition to noblemen. And "nobleman"in this context is not simply a psychological or moral concept, it refers as well to someone who has access to a higher order of reality, more substantial, in this cultural context what is called the Dao, the fundamental principle of nature. In a way, the OI does not need consolation, he already has it: the contemplation of his value, a permanent and friendly presence, a sustained opening to the infinite, in spite of the awe it inspires in him. He is drawn in a momentum of action and creation, a peaceful torment inhabits him. Circumstances feed his motivation, they provide him with incentives for action rather than frustrating him. When for the CI, circumstances are often perceived as a foe, as an obstacle to his desires, or they are used as an explanation for his failure, to justify his impotence and feed his anger. There are also forms of in-betweenness, for those who despise radical categories, those who fear the clarity of oppositions, a dualism that forces them to make explicit choices and become conscious of their existential positioning. For example, let us think of an artist who pursues his activity of creation, but is permanently haunted by his desire of fame, or a teacher, who enjoys his teaching activity but is tormented by the lack of recognition of his work and accomplishment, or an intellectual, who invests a lot of time and energy into his work, but is permanently in quest of an "honorable" status, or a mother, who is eager to be useful to her family, but dreads to be thought of as a servant and constantly seeks manifestation of gratitude or love. Those are different examples where some ideal is mixed with preoccupations of a lesser order. When one expects some reward, some payback, it indicates that the relation to the ideal is not self-sufficient, and the existential dynamic then becomes corrupted. And it is often the case that those people present an ideal image of themselves, for others and as a form of self-delusion. They are not really conscious about their motivations, and since they try to hide them, they will lack stability and strongly react to any "message" from the outside, positive or negative, compliment or criticism, they will be confused and disturbed by any unfortunate event that would expose the reality of their scheme. They will be permanently tested by life, and depending on the strength of their ideal, this life will be more or less bearable.

A current form of entertainment as an existential modality, a prominent aspect of the surrounding culture, is what can be thought of as a desire for emotional and sentimental communion. This dynamic is favored by the rise of the Internet, which offers the almost infinite possibility of creating or finding a group in which the individual will find himself, with which he can identify. Of course, we can say that such a dynamic, such a social scheme already existed before, through political, cultural or religious movements. But let's say that it was more difficult to freely start such a process on your own, more difficult to discover it. The average individual found it less easy to establish such a community. On the one hand, it often had to pass the course of institutionalization, the acceptance of an established authority, which made the task more difficult. On the other hand, there was not necessarily a place to express opinions or participate. This is visible for example in the field of publishing, where through technical means everyone can now become their own publisher and make their work, literary, musical or other, visible to everyone, instead of being limited to their family and neighbors. Creativity is the key word of the time, the "homo faber" has given way to the "homo creator". Everyone is free to provide a public form to their subjectivity, a distraction par excellence. An egalitarian self-satisfaction that induces at the same time freedom and illusion, a very pleasant circumstance which nevertheless hides a strong aspiration to recognition.

Chapter 8

The fallacy of positive thinking

Another popular way of practicing CI is the idea of "positive thinking". It benefits from a good reputation, precisely because it sounds positive, it seems good. For these people, as an example, there are no problems but challenges, or no problems but solutions. And optimism has a good reputation, it is more pleasant than pessimism. Those "positivists" do not like criticism, they prefer praise and encouragement, and if there is criticism, it should be "positive", that is gentle and indirect.. But this insistence on remaining positive implies a denial of the "dark side" of existence, a denial of pain and finitude. As well, they often pretend to be "pragmatic", and their explanations of behaviors and phenomenon are indeed pragmatic, meaning very circumstantial and in fact apologetic.. Thus they negate the metaphysical, existential or ideological dimension of being. And they exhaust themselves in those practical, contextual and superficial rationalizations. One of the concrete problems of the positive thinker is to negate the problem, by jumping right away to the "solution", transforming the "negative" into a "positive" through some type of transvaluating term, redescribing for example a problem as a challenge, even if it means postponing the solution to the Greek calends. Thus everything becomes miraculously positive. This short circuits a general consciousness of reality, which has its dark sides, a form of self delusion. By focusing on the "solution", one does not pay enough attention to the problematic phenomenon, and the conclusion might be rather hasty. As well, solutions are often used as a cover up, proposing a rather ephemeral and superficial remedy, if not illusory. As a consequence, such a person is not ready to envisage problems without real remedy, death for example. As a result, those types of insoluble problems become quite dreadful, unbearable. Thus when facing them, they get upset. When they cannot reintegrate negative information or facts into their positive system, they get destabilized, depressed or angry. Now, one can defend such positive thinking as a healthier approach, since it is more potent and dynamic, and it can be useful, to the extent it remains conscious of the limits of such a system and if it does not practice a systematic and thoughtless positive redescription.

The general problem of positive thinking (PT) is the denial of a part of reality: reality is truncated. In fact, it does not matter if it is about a negative or a positive part, approaching reality in a partial way will always end up in disappointment and pain. Positive thinking might help people in their own personal life in a momentary way, but on a larger scale, such as society or the world, they will necessarily encounter frustration. As well, there will always be people who think and act "negatively", and it will be impossible not to be angry or frustrated with them. We could say that in order to "feel good", humans need challenge, self-confrontation. One of the consequences of overcoming oneself is a feeling of self-worth. If one insists only on being happy and looking at positive things, he will not have a sense that he has accomplished anything.

Here are different problems we can identify. PT is not preoccupied with truth. The "positivizing twist" is good because it feels good, not because it is true. But being immersed in something that is not true will necessarily give a sense of imposture, and one cannot not be somewhat conscious of it. PT takes away the energy from accomplishments: the happier you are, the more complacent you get, the less you have the need to grow. And the PT overestimates the idea of happiness. PT indicates a desire to label events as "good" or "bad", instead of viewing them as "natural" and "neutral". And wherever there is "good", there is always "bad" around the corner, as the two come together. This induces a "reactive" behavior, which lacks freedom, distance and reason. PT manifests a self-suppression: it means not allowing oneself to live a range of negative emotions or thoughts that are as well normal. It is a form of self-shaming or self-censorship, just from another direction. If we insist on telling ourself "I am fine" or "No problem", we will at some point have an impression that we are lying to ourself, and we will feel even worse. So, PT actually implies not accepting yourself. When people suffering from bad self-conception artificially try to be positive about themselves, it generally backfires: they probably feel worse about themselves after saying positive affirmations than they did before as a consequence of this degrading fictitious claim. PT can also represent a form of cowardice. Either by denying the problematic dimension of a situation in order to escape any responsibility, or by claiming that things will work out on their own, thereby avoiding any singular immediate commitment, presenting itself as a sort of calm attitude of false wisdom.

Let us take a couple of further examples. When something bad happens, such as losing your job, people tell you to "just stay positive" or "look on the bright side." While such comments are often meant to be sympathetic, they can also be a way of shutting down anything one might want to express about his painful experience. Or when we express disappointment or sadness, and someone tells us that "happiness is a choice", this suggests that if we are undergoing negative emotions, then it is our own fault for not "choosing" to be happy. And if we cannot be happy, we feel even worse.

We could conclude with a concept of "toxic positivity". Of course, one can work on his perception of the world and himself and modify his apprehension in a more positive way, but this will work in a substantial manner to the extent such a transvaluation is not used to deny the negative dimension, by maintaining a dialectical perspective, conscious of the duality of reality. In this work on one's state of mind, it is crucial to distinguish the emotional phenomenon, less controllable, and the operations of reason, more based on our free will. Any negation of negativity induces a "false positive", self-destructive, since this artificial optimism is based on a lie.

Chapter 9

Morality as imposture

One important factor of CI is propriety, a recourse to moral considerations which operate as a factor of self-censorship. These ethical imperatives, we can call them as well theoretical obligations, are generated by various modalities. They can be induced by society, by established customs or principles we learned throughout our education, or through reinforced social patterns of disapproval and castigation. They can be the product of rationalization, such as the one Kant describes in the "categorical imperative": determine your actions in accordance to a maxim that could be universalized, that would or should be universally applied. Such a rationalization can as well follow the obvious sensical rule of "Do unto others what you want them to do to you", or its corollary "Don't do unto others what you don't want them to do to you.". Although this type of moral logic very much reminds us that ethical rules are often the mere extension of pragmatic considerations: moral reasoning, as the legal system, is just a nice way to protect ourselves from others while looking like a "good" person, calculations covered with a veneer of virtue. Another source of moral duty can emanate from our feelings, from sentiments such pity, compassion, guilt, shame, sympathy, fear, remorse, etc. We should here remember the rationalist theory that feelings are mere confused ideas, very intense but rather not clear.

All those virtuous and upstanding assignments and burdens function primarily as a dynamic of prohibition. After all, why would there be rules if the type of behavior recommended by these rules were natural to us! Rules are recommendations or orders that go against our most immediate drives and instincts. Therefore, applying rules is necessarily a form of self-censorship, either by prohibiting what we would like to do, or by transforming our actions into some more acceptable way, which as well implies a constraint, an interdiction. And as for any forbidding or barring, morality necessarily provokes tension, frustration, resentment, and occasionally anger. The most obvious manifestation of this internal affliction is the eagerness moral people manifest in their drive to impose their morality on their fellowmen, in a rather non-rejoicing way, and how the display of immorality of others profoundly indisposes and irritates them. They could be joyfully virtuous and have compassion for the poor wretches that are not as fortunate as them, being less enlightened, but that is rarely the case. They could simply set an example of their happy choice, thus arousing admiration and mimicry in their fellows. This aggressive behavior attests to something that looks like envy toward immoral people. Their compulsive and authoritarian "You should not do this", or more suggestive "I would not do this if I was you". Their high expectation on those matters, often emotional, expresses a definite resentment against those who take the outrageous liberty of following their desires, their will or their instinct. Those unscrupulous people who have the gall to trust their nature or themselves.

That is the reason why we describe morality as a form of imposture: it prohibits us from being ourselves. Of course, some will object that those moral principles can be quite internalized, that one can integrate them in a very personal way through his education and his life experience, but even then, they will remain at odds with other more natural inclinations, more primitive or wilder, less controlled impulses. This system of prohibition deeply affects the human spirit, who learns to mistrust himself and engender internal limitations. Of course, we cannot deny the importance of those moral principles and regulations as constitutive elements of social life and civilization. But we have to realize how much great enterprises, self-challenges, bold endeavors, have been prohibited by common morality, or took place in spite of moral boundaries. Plus too often, morality is reduced to very minimalistic and shallow rules such as "not bothering neighbors" or "not being noticed". Sometimes, great moral ideals are set into motion, but their greatness generally bears the consequence of breaching numerous less noble moral rules.

According to Netzsche, the worst in human behavior are petty thoughts, somber calculations and measly preoccupations. He writes that it is better to act evilly and greatly than to think pettily. This implies to not worry about the environment and circumstances, in order to act in accordance with oneself, following one's path. Anything short of that will induce despondent passions, sadness, frustration and regrets. And an inevitable envy toward those who dared. Grandeur, the aristocratic virtue, is not moral, although it is not against moral, it is just indifferent to it, it is in a way a higher order morality, not determined by interdictions, but by aspiration. It is the famous "become yourself" of this philosopher, which implies daring to go all the way in our own self, in our action upon the world. We don't want to do "good", we want to truly exist, repressing the temptation of self-repression, of self-doubt and self-criticism. And if we ever feel ashamed by our deeds, we should just accept this shame, live with it as a lawful consequence of our choices, and not be ashamed of our own shame. Just like we can be angry in order to act, but we should not be angry about our own anger. Strangely enough, such a shame about shame, such anger about our anger, would be truly immoral. Just like betraying ourselves can be considered the ultimate immoral behavior. As Pascal wrote: "True morality laughs at morality", since he viewed true morality from a spiritual level, more accessible to the heart, to our internal autentic drive, than to reason. Although one can here oppose the idea of a free and passionate reason to a cold and instrumental reason.

"What would you say if I did this?", asks our neighbor, the small-time moralist, brewing his resentment. He is a puritan, an adept of formal constraints, since the individual cannot be trusted: what drives him is suspicious. He is attempting to blackmail his interlocutor, threatening him or making him feel bad. He is fundamentally a punisher. He wants to practice a barter in self-repression. His interlocutor could answer him: "Do you want to do it, then do it. If you don't want to do it, then don't do it."Go wild, run naked in the streets if it fits you, and don't worry about general approval. There is a famous story about Diogenes that can enlighten our proposal. Someone wanted to study philosophy with him. Diogenes invited him to follow him through the streets dragging a herring on a string, but the man finally threw the herring and ran away, giving up his apprenticeship. Nietzsche compares petty thinking to a boil, a painful infected swelling under the skin, which itches, irritates and breaks forth. "Like infection is the petty thought: it creeps and hides, and wants to be nowhere, until the whole body is decayed and withered by this petty infection."And he explains that "The delight in petty evils spars one many a great evil deed." Thus one should not wish to be sparing. "Behold, I am disease" says the evil deed: that is its honorableness."

One interesting feature of morality as self-repression is the idea of temperance, of prudence, of circumspection. The famous aristotelian principle of the "right middle" or even the "golden middle", so familiar and pleasant to common sense, neither too much nor too little. A reasonable doctrine that is rather tempting for the meeks and the wise, since indeed it can make sense as a recipe for avoiding problems. The idea that the right path is the one between excesses, some type of balance or equilibrium. Nevertheless, like any principle it becomes problematic and even self-destructive when it is established as an absolute. For even if this axiom seems obvious and self-justified, it should not be radicalized and taken as an absolute: ironically, there should not be too much of the "right middle". Excessive prudence would be contrary to prudence, since prudence indicates a sensible and careful attitude when you make judgements and take decisions. It would become a caricature of prudence: instead of being a behavior that avoids unnecessary risks, it easily becomes a behavior that avoids any risks, a weakling attitude. And if prudence is prudent about itself, it needs something that can counterbalance it, for example passion. Passion is fed by excess, it has little concern with the convoluted calculations of our mind, such as excessive and anxious speculation on the negative consequences of our actions. Dostoievsky for example warns us against rationality and its reasonable moralism. He claims we have a need for the foolishness of transcendence, faith and the commitment it engenders. For him, enlightenment and modernity is fundamentally flawed, science and knowledge does not help us fundamentally with our lives, neither to provide happiness nor meaning. The causes of substantial human actions are beyond any accounting and explanations of them. He claims that our anxiety is largely caused because we are forced or expected to be measured in our thoughts and actions, because we are forced to conform to some institutional rationalism in order to feel reassured. The same barbarian institutional conformism that Kafka criticizes in his works, for example. Rationality, common morality, just as technology and science make our life assuredly more convenient, so we are led to believe that we can manufacture happiness through well calculated formulas, procedures and techniques. "It is life that matters, nothing but life, the process of discovering, the everlasting and perpetual process." Therefore we should be suspicious about any algorithms or principles that are supposed to provide us with well-being and happiness, an easy form of unconscious existential imposture. If there is happiness, it surges as a by-product of what we do, it cannot be predefined as a goal. Therefore is it judicious to be a fool, to transgress established rules, we should trust our passion and allow ourselves to be fools. Although we should here specify that reason, just as morality, is often taken in a reductionist way, as a formal and instrumental procedure, rather than in a broader and more free sense of the higher faculty of human creativity. Reason, as Dostievsky described it and criticized it, has a merely regulatory nature and function, and therefore can be denounced as a means for a circumstantial imposture. But reason, in a broader sense, rather taken as an impetus and assertion, as a power to exist, corresponds more to an ontological imposture, since any such daring affirmation or impetus confronts itself to the absolute and not to some established principle that it has to please and abide by.

Let us now approach the moral imposture through the bias of satisfaction and dissatisfaction. Let us propose the following idea. The righteous man can never be fully satisfied with his action and glorify himself, because eternally facing the misfortunes of the world is unbearable to him, so he does not rest on the good he thinks he is doing. He is aware of being the cause or part of this misfortune of the world. Indeed, either he evaluates his action in its proper measure, so measly in the face of reality, however immense the latter may be, or he compares his accomplishment to the circumstances, mainly to the actions of others that he can observe, or he evaluates them by the recognition he obtains. This does not mean that he cannot have a certain contentment with himself, but simply that he should never lose sight of the finitude of his actions; he cannot take pride in it, it would be ridiculous in view of the reality.

The main reason for this ban on self-satisfaction does not seem to us to be moral, although we can refer to it if we are adept of such a value system, by a simple critique of the pride and narcissism involved in this posture. The criticism can also be of an ontological order, by placing things at their fair value, in the light of universality, by realizing the miserable dimension of our actions and the immensity of the remaining task. But after all, why not be satisfied with finitude, one could object. Nevertheless, it seems more interesting to us to consider the psychological dimension of the affair. Let us start from the principle that any satisfaction tends to wish to perpetuate itself, not to wither, or even more, it wants to amplify. As well, the morally satisfied individual wants to eternally receive the wages of his action, he wants to receive a permanent recognition for it. This expectation makes him sensitive, vulnerable, it puts him at the mercy of other people's moods. However, he encounters a double difficulty. He is already in competition with this other, in relation to whom our subject is his own eyes "visibly more moral", an attitude which can arouse antagonism and jealousy, as in any competition. But he also expects this other to applaud and congratulate him, and even more than his criticism, he fears his indifference: he must be recognized. On the other hand, he worked hard to carry out his moral action, he made efforts, he sacrificed his immediate pleasure and interests, he took it upon himself. Thus anyone who does not try to imitate him, who does not see him as a model, who does not choose him as the path to follow, insults him, despises him, reduces his action to nothing since he awaits the reward that will crown his enterprise. However, we can often be surprised when we observe that people who believe they are moral, who instead of remaining on their initial satisfaction and drawing calm and well-being from it, need so much the gaze of others that they get angry, that they resent those who do not honor them, that do not participate in their moral enterprise, that do not imitate them and even just disagree with them. These moralists could just look down on those "indecent"fellows, ignore them, even criticize them, but in fact they resent them and they react emotionally. If we want to push the argument further, we can here suspect a form of envy. It is the resentment of those who work hard in relation to the shirkers, those good-for-nothings who feel no obligation to work, those who are free from any moral pressure, those who feel no need to prove themselves to others and to themselves. For all these reasons, the poor moralist feels miserable, he gets angry, he easily becomes a kind of irate and aggressive zealot. In fact, those who feel like moral beings actually grant themselves power, by virtue of this hard-won moral authority, and they want to exercise their power. We see it, for example, in the fervent followers of laws and the regulations, who feel imbued with an ultimate power, who have a right and must impose it on everyone, with mortuary and anger. Dostoyevsky calls this "administrative ardor", which obviously he makes fun of, visible in particular among those who have found there a way of identifying themselves, of making themselves unique. So this is the price to pay for the moral imposture, this morality which does not know how to laugh at itself, to paraphrase Pascal's principle.

Chapter 10

Envy as imposture

Envy is an emotion which occurs when a person lacks - or feels the lack of - another's superior qualities, achievements or possessions, and either desires it or wishes that this other be deprived of it. Envy is one of the most potent causes of human misery. Aristotle defined envy as pain at the sight of another's good fortune, stirred by the existence of "those who have what we ought to have". It is precisely in the "ought to have" that we encounter the imposture, the pretension. For some strange reason, this is mine, it legitimately goes to me, but it was taken away from me or not given to me; someone else stole it from me, or received it in a usurped way. The idea of "meriting it" implies that fundamentally it is mine, lawfully, almost ontologically, but empirically it is not the case. Therefore we have a claim upon what we don't have, we own what is not ours. And of course, in this process, we cannot not encounter doubts about this ownership, since it was not in fact granted to us, and from this insinuates itself in our soul the feeling of imposture.

We should here specify that envy, if it is conscious and measured, does not necessarily lead to imposture, since one does not claim some ownership but simply looks toward the other with a desire of ownership: 'I wish I had this, like him". This state might constitute a source of emulation, rather than resentment. We don't necessarily want to take away from this person what he has, we just wish we had it, without pretending that we already a priori deserve it. It implies action, and not complaint or impotence. Actually, the origin of the word "zeal", meaning great energy or enthusiasm in pursuit of a cause or objective, comes from the ancient Greek word "Zelos", the name of the personified spirit or daimon of envy and rivalry, emulation, jealousy, ardor and zeal. He was one of the powerful winged enforcers of Zeus, the king God, along with his siblings Nike (Victory), Bia (Force) and Kratos (strength). He is sometimes identified with Agon, the spirit of contest and confrontation worshiped at Olympia, the venue of the competitive games. Thus envy can represent an important source of energy and action in order to accomplish and improve ourself.

Some languages, such as Dutch, distinguish between "benign envy" (benijden) and "malicious envy" (afgunst). The former involves recognition that the other is better-off, which causes the person to aspire to be as good as him, while the latter causes the envious person to want to bring down the better-off, even at his own cost. Thus the German language uses the term "schadenfreude" to indicate taking pleasure in the misfortune of others, easily related to envy. We can observe this phenomenon when common people rejoice at the misfortunes of celebrities, or the spitefulness frequently expressed by children. Both forms, benign and malicious, can be called negative emotions in the sense that they produce some pain, but we can notice that the first case can more easily be sublimated than the second in a positive and productive psychological feature. Benign envy may lead a person to work harder to achieve more success.

An interesting observation by psychologists is that envy, as an emotion, attitude or behavior, has a structure parallel to what is called in English "gloating". This term, untranslatable in numerous languages, is defined as "dwelling on one's own success or another's misfortune with smugness or malignant pleasure". This proximity tends to support our claim of circumstantial imposture, as for envy, since this "gloating" implies to be in competition with others, in a direct or indirect way, therefore to derive our happiness from having what others do not have, which implies to determine our satisfaction or dissatisfaction by comparing ourself to others. Indeed, even if we do not compare ourselves to someone specific, we do not boast about what everyone does, about what everyone is, or about what everyone holds, but we boast about what puts us above these others, we boast about something special or extraordinary. There is therefore a competition of prerogative, of ownership, of power, etc. Likewise when we rejoice in the suffering, failures or lacks of others. In fact, "gloating" is the mirror image of envy: the latter indicates the suffering of not having what others have or the desire for their unhappiness, the former indicates the exultation of having what others do not have. or of having the satisfaction to contemplate their misfortune.

We should specify that an important feature of envy, as it implies a desire of "depriving others", is the shrinking of the soul. We do not think in terms of enlarging, of developing, of giving, but in the opposite, an attitude which engenders a shriveling of our world vision and personal state, a reduction. In a way, we can add that even though the feeling of envy might target some specific persons, even if it might crystallize itself on some particular individual relation, it is first of all a general state of mind, a certain propension of the being. It is a sentiment of injustice in our relation to the world, an unfairness, the conviction that we are not rewarded according to our merit or value, and the resentment this perception engenders is ready to channel itself at any occasion on some specific opportunity, like a predator permanently looking for a prey. In some moments it can remain as a residual or latent state, rather unfocused and undetermined in its object, nevertheless acute and intense, ready to appear. For example entertaining a cynical or misanthropic worldview, or diverse other forms of manifestation of disappointment towards reality. That is why some persons can actually be quite envious and not even realize it, or even deny it when it is brought to their attention, since they are quite occupied with their contempt and derision of the world.

Meanness is a good example of disguised envy. There is in itself no reason to be nasty, except in some pathological sadism. Socrates even claims that there is not meanness but only ignorance: not knowing where the good is, being mistaken about the goal we pursue. We would add that this ignorance is caused by some deviation of the mind, since when it desires something good and does not obtain it, it focuses on the lucky ones who have it, or are suspected to have it, and it becomes obsessed by them, envies them, it wants to hurt them. Or when the mind feels globally frustrated by its desire, any particular person will represent this ungrateful or unfair world, since each individual fails to provide him with the expected satisfaction. As well, we will notice that such persons are rather sensitive to compliments, even though they will deny such a fact or even reject those compliments, an act of supreme envy with aristocratic pretensions. The feeling of betrayal is as well connected to envy, because when we lose loyalty or attachment, it implies that someone else gets what we had, or can get it. This explains why jealousy and envy are often interchanged or used indiscriminately, being very close to each other.

Jealousy is an anger grounded in the loss - or fear of loss - of what we detain to the benefit of someone else, and envy is the anger of not detaining our « legitimate » property to someone else whom we then envy. And the mind naturally compares, compulsively: it cannot help but look at the lucky ones who have what we desire and are deprived of, one of the main causes of human misery. The other is the "chosen one", and not me, a rather unfair and sad state of reality.

One striking expression of envy in relation to meanness, is that an individual affected by an acute sentiment of envy experiences a permanent pain in his relation to other people. Everything in them reminds him of his worthlessness feeling and his suffering, in particular when those people seem satisfied or happy. That is the essence of misanthropy, when one envies universally, without any particular object to envy, without anyone particular to envy: the whole of humanity is its object. Envy radically inhabits such an individual, it is ingrained in him, an undifferentiated unspecified envy, which makes the envy totally unconscious and blind about itself. In fact, if such a person is told that he envies someone else, he will get indignant or laugh angrily, sincerely believing that he cannot envy those persons he profoundly despises, all those people with their imbecile satisfaction, plunged into the fatuity of their corrupt enjoyment. No redemption is possible, neither for himself, nor for others. His soul is permanently foaming, a rage more or less controlled, hot or icy, a moral agitation which constitutes the essence of meanness. Of course he becomes relatively incapable of explaining rationally what bothers him about these other people: he is enraged, he just wants to bite. Uncontrolled, envy grows, it operates in all directions. Gradually, devoid of a specific object, it becomes terribly intrusive, just as much as it is unconscious. It takes on the appearance of wickedness, resentment, even disgust for others and for oneself.

Funnily enough, only a passionate idealist can undergo such a state, a spirit full of expectations, profoundly disappointed by reality and by himself. The cynic always remains an idealist, conscious or not, peaceful or rageful. Let us add, however, that both cynicism and misanthropy can be a legitimate philosophical attitude and not necessarily the result of a pathological disposition. The difference will be in nurturing the possibility of a capacity for joy or power of being, in thinking or interacting with the world. The philosophical misanthrope or cynic accepts the constraints and the reality of the world, even if he does not appreciate them. He will not pretend to radically exclude himself, he still considers himself affected by what he criticizes, but he plays his part anyway, aware of the problem, of his own shortcomings. It is in this sense that he is an ontological impostor. While the envious misanthrope or cynic is cantankerous, withdrawn into himself; he claims to be above the world or outside the world, which makes him a circumstantial impostor, who uses what he denounces in others in order to feel "better", thus becoming powerless.

Envy can be about material advantages, status, relations, popularity, fame, physical and intellectual qualities, achievements, possessions of any kind, but it generally focuses on empirical visible elements, rather superficial. This feature is quite visible in adolescents, who experience insecure identity, where the simple possession of an object like a pair of shoes or a telephone will constitute in itself an important issue. One will therefore pretend to outdo or undo the rival's advantage. The envious experiences an overwhelming painful emotion due to someone else owning desirable items that they do not possess. It generally indicates a lack of self-worth and a poor well-being. Thus the attempt to compensate by pretending, inventing for himself a "right to". Envy is not simply a desire. It is a need that originates from a strong sense of emptiness inside oneself. In a way, one has to be blind not to perceive this emptiness, of course, but envy precisely arises from a selective blindness. "Invidia", the Latin word for envy, translates literally as "nonsight", and in the Divine comedy, Dante describes blindness of the envious, their eyelids sewn shut with iron wire. They are blind to their own reality, for one to what they have already, that they do not see and do not appreciate, then to what they do not have since they pretend to own it, really or virtually. Comparing oneself is a universal aspect of human nature, the problem arises when this comparison becomes obsessional, accompanied by pain and anger, thus inciting the person to become an CI in order to alleviate or compensate for the pain. It does not correspond to the profile of the OI since, as Kant identified it, envy does not focus on intrinsic worth of our own being, on the ontological dimension, but on how it compares with that of others, the circumstantial reality.

In the CI, there is as well a conviction that satisfying envy will calm the ontological anguish he suffers from. "If I had this or that, like this other person, then my life would be quite different, much more satisfying". "If only···, like those lucky people, then things would definitely not be the same···"This is what corporations feed on when they advertise, when they set up their online stores and celebrate any new order placed. We suspect, as the advertising suggests to us, that if we buy a certain product - which is presented to us not as a mere commercial product but as the symbol of a different lifestyle - that we will be happy: our feeling of depression or meaninglessness will be solved. Perfume ads set a whole environment, in slow motion, with violins playing, of being in a field in the golden hour, laughing and kissing your true love. The scene lulls the watcher into an emotional trace, intending to invoke a sense of envy just to suggest an easy way of satisfying existential troubles and anguish; just buy this bottle, and you too can be carefree and in love, just like this person on the screen. The envy provokes the urge.

Envy engenders an impulse to imitate. For example the use of certain terms, the reference to a common place, even the common enthusiasm or the common rejection, we want to be part of it, not to be left behind or excluded. Through this community of posture or words, we will obtain that instant "everyone", and we precisely envy this "everyone", we do not want to be outdone.

Admittedly, one could argue that advertising does not care so much about the problem of envy, quite the contrary, since it is a matter of selling a product and providing everyone free access to acquire this product, by means of finance or some barter of course, and that could rather be called mimetism or imitation. Mimetism is defined as: the behavior of one who more or less unconsciously reproduces the attitudes, language, ideas of the surrounding environment or of another individual to whom he wants to resemble, and by extension any phenomenon of more or less voluntary resemblance, of communion, of identification with a model. There is a great resemblance between mimetism and envy, except that the former does not in itself imply competition with others, unlike envy. Certainly, we can find a certain emulation in mimetism, but we do not position ourselves in an attitude of conflict with what is imitated and admired. For example, in the relationship between child and parent or student and teacher. But we know that over time this kind of relationship necessarily changes, tending towards a desire of overturning the relation of subordination, a rather legitimate aspiration; to grow up is to betray. Heroes and gods are subject to fall from their pedestals as they no longer meet the needs of their admirer, and they will be hated or despised for the illusion they have fostered, willy-nilly. Although mythical models are less likely to arouse envy, since one does not really compete with them. Moreover, it is they who can most favor the ontological imposture, since their ideality and their transcendent nature authorize and promote the subject's awareness of his finitude. For advertising, envy can be embedded in the feeling of impossibility or helplessness in the face of the image or product being conveyed, especially for material reasons.

Mimetism implies free action, envy implies a feeling of impossibility, of frustration. Mimetism does not exclude sharing, envy tends to exclude or deprive, hence the spirit of competition and exclusivity. We want to have, we want the other not to have, even though this competition is not openly admitted. Even in the desire for equality, a mutual and constructed mimetism that appears universally fair, it is really about preventing anyone from "overtaking". The fight for equality is very often a personal claim, to guarantee one's own position, one's own recognition, one's own status, the only one truly legitimate, the one that is our real concern. Academic conferences are an interesting example of this, where each one in turn will get his moment of glory. No one really listens, no substantial dialogue is established, criticism is relatively banished, it simply celebrates the right to exist and to be formally honored.

According to René Girard, the infernal triangle of mimetic desire is formed by an object, an envious person who desires the goods of others, and a jealous person who protects his own goods. And the model, the one who possesses, without even wanting or knowing it, can prevent me from owning the object of my desire by appropriating it. And the being who prevents us from satisfying a desire that he himself has suggested to us becomes an object of hatred. Although he who hates hates himself first of all, because of the secret admiration concealed in his hate. Envy always harbors a fear or a sense of impotence, hence its emotional nature and high sensitivity, the suspicion of "I'll never make it", while mimetism is more serene and tranquil, although it easily slides on the side of envy.

In Buddhism, the term "irshya", meaning either envy or jealousy, is defined as a state of mind in which one is highly agitated to obtain wealth and honor for oneself, but is unable to bear the excellence of others, and therefore excellence in general, from which a denial of fundamental existential or ontological issues. In Roman Catholicism, envy is categorized as one of the seven deadly sins, the capital vices. The Book of Genesis denounces it as the motivation behind Cain murdering his brother Abel, as Cain envied Abel because God favored Abel's sacrifice over Cain's. Therefore, Cain did not dare look at the reason for God's preference, which probably would be too challenging for himself, he prefered annihilating the circumstantial manifestation of the problem. This envy is among the qualities that defile a person. "He who is glad at calamity will not go unpunished", said Solomon. Envy ruins the body's health, making bones rot and prohibiting the inheritance of the kingdom of God, since one is focused on his own selfish passions and pleasures instead of God's will or justice. In Islam, envy is an impurity of the heart which can destroy even one's good deeds, since one must be content with what God has willed and believe in the justice of the creator. A good Muslim should not allow his envy to desire or inflict harm upon the envied person. One important characteristic we should add is that envy is often passionate, therefore a source of blindness and obsession. Like in love, we are fascinated with the other, with a mixture of admiration and scorn, of desire and hate. From a neurobiological standpoint, apparently, the hormonal reaction to hate, jealousy or envy is the same as the one we have from being in love. So, we are as attached to the person we envy as to the one we are in love with.

Thus envy is a manifestation of a sense of imposture. The main reason being that we pretend virtual ownership of something we do not possess while it is possessed by someone else, convinced that it is legitimately ours; in opposition to this fraudulent being, we therefore deserve it. We then lose sight of any more substantial perspective and focus on mere appearances, a blindness accompanied by anger, resentment and pain. Jealousy enters as well in this description, which describes a feeling of protectiveness, insecurity or anxiety one has over a rivalry, being replaced, cheated or robbed of something or someone we possess or claim to possess. The dynamic is basically the same: a pretension to ownership of things or beings, and a competition with others. From which the imposture of owning and even worse, the imposture of the mere possibility of owning, for example in the "possession" of a person. We lose any sense of ideal or accomplishment, favoring the immediacy of satisfying our primitive needs, a self-destructive and other-destructive unconscious pattern. We prefer not to clearly establish our own existential purpose, which would force us to examine our own difficulties in realizing it, and rather focus on comparing ourselves and rivaling with others, transforming our life in a permanent competition, a very superficial and illusory scheme, characteristic of the circumstantial impostor. Although one can claim that envy in reality has nothing to do with the context, nothing to do with the outside or with others, it primarily rests upon a self-disatisfaction, a frustration with our own finitude. The context remains a mere opportunity to articulate and express this discontentment. It seems easier and less painful to formulate our anguish in a relational or comparative way, more so than in an ontological way, in relation to one's own being.

There is another interesting form of envy, expressed as a concept of self-envy, mostly used for children as a way to explain a type of psychological disorder, which has as well an interesting more general existential dimension. It is basically the dynamic of a divided inner world, a rather common occurrence. It happens when a part of the self admires another part that it cannot match. For example because it can be more free, more creative or more generous. Thus the subject feels alienated, inferior and inadequate. But he will not avow to himself the problem, since it would be to admit that at that immediate moment he is lacking this quality. So he will justify its present state and criticize or hate that other part of himself, finding it stupid, weak, irresponsible or infantile. For example the disappointed lover, the one who regrets having loved: "How could I have been so stupid!" It will despise action, thoughts or decisions that were taken in that other moment, it experiences self-reproaching, regret and resentment against itself, when it should on the contrary admire itself. But it is not psychologically ready to accept this self-challenge in the present state, it merely experiences anger and violence, like in front of someone who can do what we cannot do . This phenomenon helps us as well to understand how we can be envious of someone else, but we cannot admit this envy, so we just find emotional and warped reasons to despise and criticize this person. It is very much the case for example when people animated with a strong formal and moral scheme envy someone who is more free, but will denounce his irresponsibility, his immorality, his chaos, his lack of respect for the established order, when in fact one is envious of his freedom and creativity. The Idiot of Dostoevsky is an interesting case of this phenomenon, where the calculating and sordid members of the good society prefer to scorn the Idiot for his awkwardness and stupidity rather than admitting to themselves the beauty and generosity of his character. We can perceive the imposture of such a scheme, since we are not willing to face our own shortcomings and we prefer to attack and symbolically destroy anyone who embodies the opposite qualities, including in ourselves. The transcendent self is under attack by the menial and shriveled empirical self, falling into a scheme of circumstantial imposture, since one is focusing on criticizing another person or another part of the self as a way to avoid facing the ideal.

One noticeable manifestation of self-envy occurs through the practice of social media, a behavior that is more and more visible in our society, among other places in the consulting room of psychologists. The initial principle is that individuals cannot achieve the lifestyle or produce the image that others apparently display, they become envious, they live a life of comparison. In the past, people might have just envied their banal immediate neighbors, but now they can compare themselves with everyone across the world, they are tempted by an infinity of individuals who compete to produce the best image possible on different networks. Although the actual principle is actually to recruit an increasing number of followers, since the more followers, the more influence, the more companies will pay them to endorse their products in a post. So they are actively trying to create this desirable aesthetic, this envy of lifestyle, and get more people to sign up to see it, which implies a form of competition.. Some specialists speak of a pathological phenomenon they call "comparisonitis". If intellectually or rationally one can understand the facticity of such schemes, emotionally it still produces an effect on the psychology of the user. If those images or narratives tap into what we aspire to but what we don' t have, then it becomes very powerful.

Then an added phenomenon occurs, even more pernicious. In order to compete and produce his own artificial self, the individual constructs his own online myth, either exaggerating and twisting some positive features of his life, or outrightly inventing situations or events. They fabricate some sort of enhanced simulacrum or avatar of their existence, to which they become attached and end up believing. And weirdly, since they are periodically forced to realize that their actual life is quite different and inferior to this synthetic production, they start hating this image, out of envy. The basic dynamic is then "I deserve to be like him", or "Why am I not like him!", the subject undergoing a strong feeling of missing out and failure. In the past, such phenomenon occurred, as identified for example in bovarism, referring to the romantic heroine of Flaubert Mme Bovary. But with the help of technology, such mythologizing of our life becomes easier, more tempting and more powerful, since being visibly objectified, and being witnessed by the crowds. We actually don't measure up to the lives we tell others we are living, we look at this constructed self as though it were another person, and we feel envious of him. This creates an alienating sense of self-envy inside us, thus we feel inauthentic, curiously envious of our own avatars. It is understandable that such individuals are tempted to escape reality and to immerse themselves completely in a virtual life.

In this same pattern, we find the unhealthy desire for equality that we have already discussed, a self-justified form of envy. Envy towards the powerful, towards the rich, towards the famous, towards the best, and even towards loved ones. It takes different forms, one of them is a drive called the "tall poppy" syndrome. It is a cultural phenomenon in which people hold back, criticize or sabotage those who achieve or appear to achieve some success, especially intellectually or culturally. It describes a tendency towards mediocrity and conformity, as everyone tries to belittle others for their accomplishments, due to their own insecurities. Since we cannot embody a given quality, or for fear of not being on par with whoever holds it, we speak and act, often with anger, in order to prevent anyone from "standing out": such a possibility would make us become aware of our own incapacity. It's a form of spite: "If I can't have it, no one will have it!". This is often the case when someone is more free, more powerful, more daring or more creative. A way will be found to prohibit or curb such a manifestation of superiority, often by describing it in a negative or scornful way, rather than meet the challenge it represents. Morality is a very useful tool for this prohibition, since through the very honorable demand for equality, it provides a "good" image or cover for the envious, promoting a stifling formalism. We must bring the other to our level, lower him, otherwise we would have to "go up", a prospect that is too difficult, painful for fear of failure. So we live in a frenzy of revenge against anyone who threatens our conception of ourselves, a paradoxically comfortable and dissatisfied state.

We could state that desire for equality is suppressed envy, or a sublimation of envy, a transformation intended to make it look more positive, more acceptable, even more noble. In fact, it even looks generous, disinterested and unselfish, since we seem to be concerned about other people, when in fact the issue is generally taken very personally. The best proof of such a personal investment is the emotional dimension embodied in any such righteous claim, rather rageful. Or by observing the way such egalitarianism, in different forms or tonalities, is forcefully imposed in some groups or cultures. Of course, we observe as well in history how the thirst for equality can modify society, at the origin of many social improvements. But on a psychological level, the expectation or demand for equality often proceeds from a sense of humiliation, of worthlessness, of vanity, a combination of fear, resentment and aspiration. We should remember that vanity is a paradoxical term, which on one side denotes and excessive pride in or admiration of one's own appearance or achievements, like in "this compliment flatters his vanity", and at the same the quality of being worthless or futile, like in "the vanity of human pretensions" . These opposite meanings combine very well with the instability conveyed by the dynamic of envy, largely grounded on circumstances and the base of the comparison. The fundamental narcissistic lodged in the heart of the individual expresses itself both in the desire for praise and recognition and in the allergy to anything reminding him of his finiteness. This explains why some persons considered shy or submissive suddenly explode in some rageful or excessive demands. It's all about opportunities with the circumstantial impostor.

Another classical form of envy is expressed by those who fear making mistakes, those called perfectionists, who are both pretentious and envious. They are pretentious, since they actually believe they can incarnate some form of perfection, they unconsciously pretend they can be perfect, and in a warped way, a type of wishful thinking, they believe they are perfect. Of course, if we criticize them for such a foolish idea, they will protest, they will object that perfection is impossible, that mistakes are human, that no one is perfect, that we learn from our mistakes, etc. After all, to pretend to be perfect is a mistake! And they sincerely believe those words when they pronounce them. But like always with sincerity, it is highly suspicious. In fact, if their reason allows them to think more realistically, reasonably, and rationally, and therefore accept the idea of mistake, it is not the case with their being. Their intimate self, more emotional, more primitive, has a profound abhorrence for any manifest error, an epidermal aversion to any omission or oversight, anything that could reveal some ignorance, incapacity or stupidity. Their being therefore phantasmastically pretends to some vague and absolute idea of perfection.

Furthermore, they are envious. Probably unconsciously, but they have in their mind the image of some "faultless individual", an experience coming from school, from family or from their adult life. Since no matter how hard we try and succeed, we know there is always someone better, someone who is successful when we fail, someone who is more competent and more worthy than us, someone who does not make the mistakes we make. This faceless, indentityless individual who never makes mistakes haunts like a ghost the mind of the perfectionist, although sometimes, even worse, it might have a shape and a name. It is this stare that makes him blush when he realizes his own flaws and errors, when he gets caught red-handed making a blunder, or at the mere idea of doing it. It is that imaginary ruthless, pitiless and cruel gaze which acts as his conscience, imposing itself as his regulatory ideal. Somewhat like a parental figure we both admire and envy, and that we hate because we bear in our soul the conviction that we will never be as good as "it", we will never be good enough for "it". This ectoplasm is the embodiment of our existential suffering, of our flaws and limits, and with it we compete when we pretend to be perfect, when we angrily jump at the slightest criticism from anyone, when we vehemently attempt to justify ourselves or defend ourselves, even preemptively, before being criticized. We are envious and we don't know it, and we don't even want to know: it would look too ridiculous.

In annex, we should mention an interesting feature of the perfectionist, what is called secondhand shame, vicarious or indirect shame, or more recently named spanish shame. It is the shame we suffer from when someone else does something we consider shameful, in this case someone making mistakes. We take it very personally, we even get angry at those mistaken people, a common phenomenon with teachers or parents. It is as if the perfectionist wanted to annihilate any reminder of human imperfection, especially in his immediate surroundings, or in his area of responsibility. Mistakes, not under my watch! Not when I am watching, the sight is too painful···We can generally identify in this scheme an idea of hard work and sacrifice, on the altar of perfection, and anxious worry about appearance. "If I suffer, you should suffer as well". Observing mistakes is painful for the perfectionist, but unbearable are those people who do not even care about it, those who are fine with their mistakes, those that ignore the very idea of mistakes, those who are not interested in the principle of sacrifice. Especially when those nincompoops happen to be more successful, more recognized or happier than them, an occurrence which unfortunately happens frequently. Strangely, there is a double envy. The one against perfect people, even if they don't exist, and the one against those who don't care about mistakes, who are satisfied with themselves. This is the same mechanism by which moral people get angry with immoral people, instead of just having pity and compassion for them. They are aware of both their lack and their anxiety. It is understandable why they focus on the circumstances, rather than worrying about their being.

Chapter 11

The imposture of transcendence

We could say that the most primitive passion in a human being is the animal passion: the desire to survive, which includes primarily the instincts of nourishment, of protection, of mating and reproduction. A fundamental and crucial drive that makes us stay alive and persevere in our being, as Spinoza identified it with his concept of conatus. But it seems to us that reducing our life to this biological dimension is not sufficient or adequate to explicate human existence, which needs values, goals and endeavors in order to provide a necessary meaning to his being. This explains for example the phenomenon of religion or intellectual activity. The access to something that transcends our corporeal being, an ontological dimension that allows us to deal with our sense of finitude. Otherwise, as we have explained at length, one falls in the endless and frustrating trap of competition and comparison, what we called circumstantial imposture. Therefore the human needs to discover and experience within himself this added dimension of passion which goes beyond a mere desire to survive and can even go against it, since this "new" human passion can come in conflict with and take precedence over the desire to survive. The passion that emerges can be of social or personal nature, it can be moral, existential, aesthetic, spiritual, political, intellectual, etc. We can observe this feature very early in the history of human existence, for example with the production of ornaments, the cave paintings, the work on astronomy and astrology, the writing, in parallel with the development of practical instruments needed for agriculture, manufacture, hunting or combat. And what is true for human history is true for individual history, since according to the famous principle, ontogeny recapitulates phylogeny. This passion can take a very active form, with purely external manifestation, in relation to society or the world, but it can be moved as well by an interiorized ideal. It can be quite emotional, but it can also take a meditative form, calm and collected, internal and personal, hardly visible from the outside, except through some rituals. Let us call this latter form a passion for transcendence, which implies a certain disconnection from the empirical world, an estrangement or abandonment of the biological or survival mode that can be called detachment. Although the ideal that generates a worldly activity can as well be related to some form of transcendence.

Nevertheless, the search for detachment is in a way a natural process for the human, because life is hard, because we suffer, because we need meaning, because our mind is attracted and lured by the infinite. Thus someone who has a hard time with life searches for a way to be detached from his daily occupations and preoccupations, he then looks for something, some thinking or activity that would facilitate this detachment. In another period, traditional religion was the obvious way to go for such a quest, but nowadays in the west, popular techniques and exercises are meditation, breathing, yoga, and other various spiritual practices connected to "new-age" trends, with its trail of self-help and psychological theories. We here use this concept of "new-age", already vague in itself, more as a symbol than a concrete reality. It indicates a mixture of esoteric pursuits, orientalism, new spiritualities, a glorification of body, feelings and emotions, what can be called a holistic approach to self and the world. We can encounter as well a fascination with weakness and vulnerability, an admiration with childhood, a suspicion toward science and technology, a fear of pain and discomfort, a glorification of well-being and happiness, a reversal from "masculine" to "feminine" values (for example interpersonal caring in opposition to heroism). All these features have in common an anti-rationality perspective or at least a doubtful attitude toward it. Although in this phenomenon, being a mere tendency rather than a clear cut ideology, we will encounter numerous and quite different variants of it, even contradictory ones.

But playing with transcendence is a risky business. Transcendence can become an imposture, a circumstancial imposture, when it is used as a mere stratagem to deny reality. An individual, caught in the routine of comfort and survival, unsatisfied, discovers one day some type of faith, of initiation, of wisdom, that challenges his established life habit. He finds in it, as a belief and a practice, some content that provides a renewed meaning to his life. He gets involved in his new existential system, but slowly, without realizing what is taking place, he gets installed in it, he establishes a new pattern of comfort. After all, comfort, in its etymology, is what makes us stronger, what supports us, as the radical "fort" indicates, which means "strong". Once we are strong, we feel confident, at ease, protected, and from then on we can feel good about ourselves, since nothing can disturb or threaten us, hence the idea of comfort and the satisfaction that comes with it. What used to be a challenge for the self can, as an acquired nature, becomes a resting seat, an agreeable and secure setting, from which one can look triumphantly at the world, gloat and feel good. From the standpoint of detachment, what was a process of challenge, criticism and distance becomes a new way to validate oneself. One can therefore say that such an individual cannot detach himself from his detachment, since his detachment has become a new attachment. The former detachment process has become a new form of alienation, just by switching the landmarks. The same way he was attached and grounded in his survival mode, he is now attached and grounded in his transcendent mode, which then becomes a new form of survival, since it has become a need to be satisfied, a new form of self-satisfaction, a new way to value oneself. The transcendence, captured and established, ceases to be an actual and active transcendence, it becomes a ghost of itself, since it has been castrated of its challenging dimension for the self: it only challenges others, since we are the masters of the doctrine, the bearer of the word. Thus it can be identified as a form of circumstantial imposture, since we believe we have reached the "holy place", we claim to detain wisdom, we pretend to be on the right side of things. We rely on an established theory, we base ourselves on other's behavior, be they the "good" people whom we imitate or the "bad" people we look down upon. The apparent detachment becomes a new type of attachment, the drive for a biological survival has become the drive for a psychological survival, but it is still a matter of survival, and absence of freedom. Thus, even though we do not wish to negate the value or interest of such transcendent values, we need to find a way to avoid falling in the trap of circumstantial imposture and identify a form of ontological imposture. In order to this, we propose the concept of "detachment from detachment", a redoubling of practice of detachment, in order to give it back its substance, its value and its dynamism.

Detachment from detachment is a paradoxical expression, which escapes immediate logic and understanding, hard to grasp. Let us take an example in order to deal with the issue and make it more visible. Imagine, or maybe we know such a person since it is today a common phenomenon, a person who is an adept of some new-age wisdom. He will engage into yoga, meditation, in some form or other of esoteric practice, generally inviting the adept to some "beyond thinking" or "beyond the mental" attitude and behavior. During this process, generally taking place in specific places and moments, he will break out of his usual routine, getting away from his usual activities, thoughts and preoccupations. We could say he interrupts the "survival mode", finding in such an exercise a form of transcendence and freedom. But without realizing it, he starts sacralizing this activity, he establishes some form of psychological dependence. He projects in this specific modality, in this specific moment and specific activity, his hopes and expectation of salvation, of peace, of satisfaction, of happiness, or whatever he is desperately looking for. Strangely enough, his investment in a given ritual develops into a new mode of survival, a new type of survival that is the mere negation of his previous or traditional survival. Negation of reason, negation of the world, negation of others, negation of any practical dimension of existence. The quest for physical and psychological comfort transformed itself into a spiritual comfort, what can be called a religious attitude. He folds in on himself, along with his belief and his new routine, he cocoons, and establishes a little world in itself, where he is the king, if not the god. Indeed, compared with the behavior of "normal" people, he does take distance and seems distant, he practices detachment. But he has fabricated a new idol, maybe even more powerful than the previous one, since it is touching some form of absolute, since he is now protected from the contingencies of reality. We can thus suspect that his apparent detachment conceals an even stronger form of attachment, like a form of intoxication, since he is under the influence of a doctrine and a new habit, engendering a new form of necessity, needing a new form of survival. This type of sublimation of the survival mode is typical of religious thinking and behavior, which makes it very difficult to discuss with a religious person: you are a believer and you see how great the belief is, or you are not a believer therefore you cannot understand. Or course, connecting belief and understanding can make sense, as Augustine claims it, since to understand a scheme implies at least momentarily to surrender to this scheme, and to suspend any critical judgment. We notice this when we read a philosophical text: in order to better understand the author, we have to accept a certain form of abandonment, we have to put aside our opinions, our beliefs, our knowledge, and even our feelings, in order to imitate or to model our thinking on the author's mental process, at least momentarily. The same is true when we want to understand another person, especially when their way of being is quite different from ours. We are then faced with a crucial choice. Do we become a convert, is this text for us a new gospel, an unquestionable doctrine? Or do we keep our distance, do we extract ourself in a second instance, in order to maintain a critical perspective and remain conscious of the limits of our new revelation. Here we can speak about a process of conversion, but it seems to us that a real dynamic of conversion has to constantly remain alive, it has to question us and be reversible, a permanent process of conversion that guarantees detachment of detachment. Otherwise we just relapse in an updated form of dogmatism, an alternative form of psychological necessity. Carl Jung wrote that the cognition is infinite, but on the way a person meets two obstacles: the external unknown and the internal unknown. The external is the world and the internal is the self or the subconscious. He has fear for the two. So he tries to balance between the two fears. And finally settles down with something that protects him both from himself and from outside

Neurophysiologists have an interesting way to describe the dogmatic phenomenon. They explain that the brain does permanent work on maintaining homeostasis. One of its tools is to understand and give meaning to what is happening, which allows us to make predictions. The better the brain predictions are, the more free energy is emitted. When the brain cannot understand what is going on, entropy rises, together with anxiety, frustration, etc. To avoid a state of disequilibrium, the brain looks for explanations that would justify that things are the way they are. Once an explanation that works is found, the brain is reluctant to modify that explanation or doubt it, as each time such a process takes energy and a state of doubt and indetermination is painful.This is why it is difficult for people to refute what they think or believe in, as they will have to start the making sense process all over again. Even if an explanation is not functioning very well, it is often considered easier to stick to it, rather than spend the energy on looking for something completely new. Brain is the most energy consuming organ, so one of the goals is to reduce this energy waste as much as possible. Yet, if one is conscious of the way the mind functions, one can deliberately master one's reactions. The more conscious one is of the way one functions, the more efficient is the mind, due to the high quality of his predictions and its acquired plasticity.

Another way to think about detachment from detachment, is that one is not merely detached from the world and from others, but one is detached as well from his own self. Like always in our philosophical work, a key issue is distance and problematization, which in order to be authentic and rigorous implies self-distance and self-problematization. And strangely enough, this detachment from detachment brings us closer to others. Availability, as Zhuangzi would say, a capacity to greet reality and act accordingly, without preconceived ideas about good and evil. Real love would say Eckhart, a love which supersedes possessive love, pure giving, agape and not eros. An interesting example of this detachment from detachment is given to us by Plato in the "allegory of the cave". He tells us about an individual who managed to escape the pain and the ignorance of living in appearance and illusions, and who after an arduous journey finally sees the "true light"of reason. He thinks that "Better to be the poor servant of a poor master"in this wonderful place rather than going back to the cave. But finally he determines that he "must be made to descend again among the prisoners in the cave, and partake of their labors and honors", as a the lawful conclusion of the process. Even if this will terminate in his own demise, since he is not fitting anymore such a context, as a form of self-surrender, being detached even from his own self. Nietzsche describes the same process with his Zarathustra, who leaves his home at the age of thirty and retreats into the mountains hoping to find enlightenment. There, "six thousand feet beyond man and time", Zarathustra remains for ten years, and in his solitude his spirit grows, he pierces into the enigma of man and existence. But one morning, tired of his solitude and overflowing with wisdom, Zarathustra decides that it is time to detach himself from his heightened consciousness, and like the setting sun, descends from his mountain to empty his wisdom into the world of ordinary men.

In order to come back to the opposition between CI and OI, it appears that this religious attitude is more than often in the order of circumstantial thinking. There are diverse reasons for this. First of all, because the subject caught in such a matrix of belief uses it in order to justify and validate himself. Since he believes, since he practices, he is "good", he is "right". Being on the upright and virtuous side of things, he is granted an a priori worth and positive value, independently of his attitude or realizations. He accomplishes the proper ritual, he pronounces the adequate speech, he therefore "knows", he is one of the initiates, unlike those other people, all those ignorants, base, pagan and mindless people. This posture somewhat reminds us of those Pharisees that the gospel highlights and criticizes, those "true believers"who are recognized because they loudly pray, being very proud of themselves since they have high religious and moral standards, but who care little about other people.

A typical password of those New age converts, often unconsciously so, is the usage and reference to the term "ego". They don't use it with the positive or neutral meaning of classical philosophy, as the expression of a thinking subject, including his limited and subjective dimension. Nor in the Freudian sense, where the ego is the voice of reason and temperance, an instance of the self operating between the primitive pulsions of the id and the formal imperatives of the superego in order to find a compromise between the demands of the outside world and the internal needs. In this new negative connotation of the term, the ego is a mixture of illusion, the inflation of our self-conception, an excessive credit to our self-importance, very much inspired by buddhism where the individual self has no real substance. The initiates therefore witness their faith by using and abusing the word "ego", with which they explain and account for most evils, miseries and wrongdoings of the world and the individual. Just like for christian believers the simple usage of the word "sin"allows to explain most human behavior and flaws, it indicates that one is on the right side of things, showing and proving his self-righteousness. It would never come to the mind of the true christian believer to take distance from and criticize the concept of "sin", no more than for the new-age believer to take distance from and criticize the concept of "ego". We call this circumstantial imposture since one does not challenge himself anymore, but merely adapts himself to a context in order to determine his thinking and his existence. He considers himself successful because he respects the rules and obeys to the established procedures, he feels good and successful by comparing himself to the ones who refuse or ignore this blessed stratagem : the bad people. In a way, if he accepted the substantial reality of the term, he could use it as an object of challenge, but this would imply distance and critical analysis of the term, a certain benevolence or understanding towards the non-initiated, a lesser pride and certainty with himself, a more thoughtful and cautious utilization of the sacred word. But with "sin"just like with "ego", it is easy to become pretentious, and through a simple password, to claim some kind of perfection by comparing ourselves to the "bad"people.That is within any religion the tempting hypocrisy of clerical behavior, the "holier than thou"attitude that characterizes the initiated people, the canonical and priestly behavior who, engrossed in their permanent preaching, end up believing that that they know, that they are honored and blessed, ideally so. We heard once one of those famous "wise"enlightened new-ager pretend he had "no more ego", a funny sentence is there is one in this domain, since he did not realize the performative contradiction of such a statement. Not only did he indulge in a strong affirmation of the "I", but he claimed for it some type of perfection that would be possible only in the very disappearance of this "I". In those moments, or in such an inclination, the subject remains a circumstantial impostor, since the infinite power of the transcendence is forgotten, while using comparison to "inferiors"and the seduction of speech in order to proclaim one's glory and complete achievement. An attitude which is generally reinforced by disgust, scorn or indignation towards those "untouchables"that have not reached or even ignore such level of wisdom.

In terms of the contemporary criticism of the traditional religious or dogmatic attitude, a mention should be made about another intellectual phenomenon of a rather different origin than the "New age" conversion , nevertheless pointing in the same direction: deconstruction. It bears a more classical philosophical foundation, primarily identified to Jacques Derrida and his inspiration in Martin Heiddegger. The point of such an approach is first of all to expose or unveil the hidden postulates or hierarchy in any discourse or attitude, often rendered invisible because it is usual and therefore considered "normal" in society, in the daily functioning of an individual, or in a culture. This « normality » can even lead us to ignore a rather biased or unfair scheme, rendering it acceptable. Deconstruction invites us to examine critically the modalities of speech. The basic dynamic of such a process often functions in a dual or antinomic relation where one of two opposite terms governs or overrides the other, axiologically or logically. Derrida identified for example how this precedence operates in different instances: signified over signifier, intelligible over sensible, speech over writing; activity over passivity, etc. He then wants to reevaluate certain classical western prejudices such as poetry versus philosophy, reason versus revelation, structure versus creativity.

The first task of deconstruction is, according to Derrida, to identify and overturn these oppositions inside the understanding of a text. Although the final objective of deconstruction is not to surpass all oppositions, because it is assumed they are structurally necessary to produce sense. The oppositions simply cannot be suspended once and for all, as the hierarchy of dual oppositions always reestablishes itself, being necessary to meaning. Deconstruction only points to the necessity of an unending analysis that can make explicit the postulates and hierarchies intrinsic to a text. But it is not enough to expose and deconstruct the way oppositions work and then stop there in a nihilistic or cynical position, since it would prevent any effective intellectual action. Derrida proposes the principle of creating new terms, not to synthesize the concepts in opposition as in Hegelian dialectics, but to mark their difference and eternal interplay. But as always, since the human mind, out of a certain inertia and a desire for immediate certitude, "knowing and saying the truth", the inheritance of Derrida has been primarily to pick up on the criticism of hidden postulates, to overturn them, and to make out of this reversal a new unquestionable dogma, sometimes in a radical and virulent form. What was an opportunity for detachment only became again the opportunity for a new attachment, as strong if not more than the previous, since new converts easily tend to be zealots. That is what we can observe for example in the crusade for political correctness in its various forms, the zealots of deconstruction, such as the extremist "cancel culture". We will probably have to wait for a new generation or two in order for the situation to calm down, or even revert itself, and probably see the emergence of a new doctrine. Although we can already notice some violent reactions to such excess.

We shall admit that these inflections or reversal of beliefs and practices are useful in themselves, they correspond as well to a normal and even legitimate shift in social values. But too often, once such a tool or belief is found, the individual clings to this relative detachment and the new attachment it provides. He becomes aggressive when those new postulates are criticized, he rejects people who are not in the same stream. Today, the phenomenon of reinforcement of personal beliefs engendered by social networks tends to intensify such a process, since any user tends to attract and follow primarily other users moved by the same vein of thought, which comforts him in his convictions. When such a subject is confronted with the opposite of what he values, he gets upset and indignant, he doesn't want to see the limits and drawbacks of his scheme, he cannot problematize it. In other words, he is now glued to the so-called detachment, since this revelation now constitutes his identity. But for true detachment, which includes detachment from detachment, one should not depend on any specific detachment, neither on detachment itself, nor on the means through which one gets detached. When the circumstantial impostor is especially dependent on such concepts or practices, as he needs a "crutch" that would support his identity and his worldview; what happens to be outside of his conceptual domain is treated either with indifference, or hostility.

True detachment, or detachment of detachment, implies self-annihilation and distance. Both are demoted nowadays in a popular culture of self-praise, an increased sensitivity to mobile external influences from diverse groups. Social media pages, our browsers, advertisements we receive, etc. are made to reinforce our existing preferences, so that the otherness is abolished: what we see daily is the duplication and reproduction of what we think we think and like. In order to create distance, there has to be the presence of otherness and a certain openness of mind. In the absence of alterity, there is a strong identification with oneself, therefore no detachment is possible. One remains identical with oneself, one is caught in a self-coincidence. For it to be otherwise, one would need to reconcile with some "not existing", a radical otherness, which turns out to be difficult, in particular for the circumstantial impostor, very determined by the presence of an immediate reality. The "other" represents for him a disturbance, a threat to his integrity, and detachment of detachment is the ultimate otherness. This otherness lies in the foundation of problematization, since in order to detach one has to problematize. In other words, to see the limits of an idea, a phenomenon or an experience, is only possible through taking distance from oneself, which is again, a great difficulty for the adept of circumstances, who firmly believes in his own perceptions. Therefore a current form of imposture, close to dogmatism, is the rigid attachment to a way of being, to a given paradigm.

What are the two main features of a paradigm shift?

First of all is "decentration". In our time, social relations move away from traditional institutions, becoming more "tribal"oriented: we identify with our peers, those who are like us, those who think like us, rather than structures in place. Individual freedom prevails over the sense of obligation, favoring personal initiative rather than integration in formal or traditional institutions. Multiplicity predominates over unity. Ethics dominate over morality, the former being more contextual and less ontologically grounded, more fluid than the latter. Organic groups replace administrative or political configurations, for example ethnic identity or affinity of interest. Seduction is favored over coercion, pleasure over duty. The world becomes a mere horizon, the local environment becomes the grounding. Reality is more fleeting, less stable.

Second is deconstruction. Rationality, considered suspicious, yields to feelings and emotions. Relations are primordial, rather than general or abstract theories, intersubjectivity prevails. Imagination and creativity dominate over rationality and logic. Spirituality and religiosity rather than established religion, what implies a personal experience rather than a tradition. The body is valued and even glorified, through physical exercising, healthy nourishment, a hygienism conceived as a morality, a willful embellishment which includes an alteration or reshaping of its conformation, which implies a strong sense of individuality. Body-engineering conceived as an expression of personal freedom, a liberation from biological determination. Letting go, freedom and pleasure, rather than commitment, playfulness and immediate satisfaction rather than arduous work and career building. The existential present predominates over the past and the future, immediacy rules. Energy is privileged above structure, for example to deal with bodily or psychological problems.A holistic worldview rather than utility, for example protection of nature overrules industrial production, at least on the ideological level. Horizontal immanence rather than vertical transcendence, which implies equality rather than hierarchy. Positive thinking rather than criticism or negativity. Virtuality is dethroning empirical reality, what can be called a fabrication or diversification of reality, the fashionable "multiverse", presented as an immediate future. Romanticism of the archaic unseats the glory of a rational modernity; one can find here a funny combination of the mythical or mystical pre-modernity and the relativistic post-modernity.

Chapter 12

The romantic imposture

The romantic impulse, drive or sensitivity is one of the most common, natural and easy ways to access transcendence, or at least trying or pretending to do so. But we could say that romanticism is a misguided love, deprived of its life substance. Let us remember that transcendence indicates a "going beyond", or a "going outside". But we cannot accomplish such an escape or overcoming without some "object" , some projection sticking out, some ontological bump or protrusion that we could catch, that we could cling to. For the newborn, his mother or whichever person is around, taking care of him, will capture the possibility of this impulse: the need for otherness, the root of desire for transcendence. There is a fundamental anguish in the closure upon the self, the experience of the finiteness of being, is a primitive and fundamental one. And of course, as most crucial experiences, it starts by being lived within the depth of our own singular being, within our "flesh". Indirect experience comes later on, as we learn to exteriorize our own being, as we discover decentering ourself.

Thus the baby, and the child, fixates on a given being as an anchoring for his existential needs. And we all have the ingrained memory of such a fundamental experience, even though it might not be conscious in our adult life. Often, for some persons, this memory is blurred by other recollections, past impressions, not so pleasant, that might even be interpreted as traumas, as numerous psychologists call them. This fusional feeling of bliss nevertheless remains present in our being, a sentiment of emotional saturation where we seem to encounter a sense of completeness. As in the ancient Greek myth, we have encountered our "lost part", we are now a complete being, nothing is now missing. This is what characterizes the romantic moment of elation. Finally, someone that loves me, someone that understands me, someone that fully accepts me, someone that seems to fulfill my most essential needs, someone that makes me feel worthy and great. Who could resist such an occurrence!

Thenceforth, in such an intense intercourse, who needs reasons, who needs reason! As Montaigne explained his great friendship with La Boétie, "Because it was him, because it was me", indeed the sole possible explanation. Although we should specify that this "love story" only lasted a few years, since La Boétie died young, a brevity and a loss which probably intensified the later perception of this relation by the author. So it is with the infatuation, with the initial mental state of a love encounter. But we should be conscious that this initial state of a love affair is in general not bound to last, it is only the strength of the first encounter, the reason why we call this phenomenon "falling in love". There is something unpredictable about it, that seems to happen by itself, since one does not "decide" to fall in love with someone specific. The term "falling" implies that there is no control of the process, that there is a loss of the self, since the events take place in spite of our will, or without any consideration for our expectations and fears. Thus one most likely will be surprised at this "falling", like in physical falling. At the same time, this extraction of ourself allows us or forces us into a daze, a strange state that alienates us from our own stability and identity, a rather anxiogenic feature, while procuring some intense pleasure, a bit like when we get drunk or take some drug. Falling in love is quite destabilizing, since it takes us out of our psychological and existential routine, with a mixture of pleasure and pain, in a rather intense and contradictory way. It is the pleasure of encountering what seems to be our "missing part", the soulmate we were longing for, and at the same time it provokes anxiety since we feel easily abandoned in its absence, or anxious, since we became heteronomous, depending in the outside, depending on someone else that we might lose, that might decide to leave us. Not even to mention the fact that this feeling is not required or may not be. Plus, with the glorification of our "partner", we easily can undergo the impression that we are not at the right level for this great person, that maybe we don't deserve such a wonderful being, or that this life miracle is not destined to remain eternally: it is too beautiful to be believed, too beautiful to be true.

In this sense we can observe a type of regression in the mind of the loving subject. Actually, his worry is not so much to love but to be loved, with the suspicion that he is not worthy of such a blessing, he is not good enough for it, he does not deserve such an "honor". This fits exactly what happens in the mind of the young child. First, as a newborn, he just wants his physical and psychological needs to be satisfied, then as he grows up and humanizes himself this transforms itself in a desire to be loved, a expectation which develops along with the anguish that "mummy might not love me any more", "mummy does not really love me today", or even the awful perspective that "mummy never loved me. We cannot avoid the residual doubt that we do not deserve the love we receive, the conviction that we are fundamentally not lovable. Initially, this relation is determined by the fact this person is the first one he meets, and is his primary caretaker. As a youth or an adult, he will more or less reject or overcome this relation, in order to project such a scheme onto a pure stranger. From this process, we can see how the love process makes the individual decenter himself, go beyond himself, and in this sense allow an access to some experience of transcendence.

But the ultimate and crucial step is often missing in the maturing process. This essential transition would be to pass from a state of wanting to be loved, to a state of loving. By wanting to be loved, the subject is still centered on himself, remaining anxious and needy. If and when he loves, he actually dies to himself, he escapes his own internal demands, in order to totally focus on the other person, or other persons, trying to provide what is required for them, by them. But he can focus on them in two different ways. In an empirical way, centered on the person itself, on his immediate desires and needs. Or in a transcendental way, centered on the fundamental aspirations of this person, on its power of being, on its existence in the "overcoming" sense of this term. Using our established distinction, he can view this person as a CI or as an OI, without evidently being conscious of such a distinction. As a CI, he will focus on making this person comfortable, he will attend to all his primitive needs. In this sense he is selfless, to the extent he has no expectations for himself, although in the absolute this attitude is a rather rare or short lived occurrence, but he does not allow or encourage the other person to be selfless. He in fact reinforces in this way the self-ishness or the primitive inclinations of this person. The lover then acts as an actor of the "warrior's rest", providing the object of his attention with satisfying compensations, encouraging his need for comfort, a common form of spiritual corruption. He offers the other a consolating scheme for the harshness of life, which on the one hand is understandable, pleasant and useful, on the other hand reductionist and complacent. Of course, as we wrote before, such a behavior is rarely gratuitous, since most lovers expect from this "investment" recognition, gratitude, love, or whatever psychological need they are eager to satisfy. The lover organizes and creates conditions that can please, appease or satiate their interlocutor, reinforcing in him the delight and importance of gratifying circumstances, even establishing a dependency.

For the OI, the perspective is rather different. We could say that for him the relationship is either a school, in the sense that both partners are there to learn from each other and improve each other, or a tatami - the mat that covers the floor in martial arts, the place of the fight - in the sense that both partners respectfully, joyfully and cordially permanently challenge each other, accompanying each other in their struggle with their respective quest of values. A good lover is a good student and a good educator, a meaningful love relation is like a classroom. Thus tension and pain should not be excluded from the process, an expectation that would be illusory and counterproductive. And we will oppose to such a dynamic the common conception of love as a "battlefield", where both partners struggle for power, competing against each other in order to satisfy their material and psychological needs. There, they seek a primitive recognition of the partner, reinforcing in each other the most crude desires and demands. The couple has generally an amplification function, intensifying either the best or the worse in both partners of the relation.

In an OI relation, conscious of the discrepancy between our being and our ideal, each partner, in his focus on the other person, which of course does not exclude to focus on himself, helps him to struggle with his own ideal. We should be conscious that in such a perspective, the lover might go against his own immediate empirical self-interest, since satisfying his needs becomes a secondary issue. There is a true selfless dimension in helping someone pursue his ideal, to the extent that it is a mutual quest, since one does not practice an exchange of "goods", a sort of bartering that implies a sordid but nevertheless common calculation of "benefits". Even though it is not explicitly avowed, one provides his support and "sacrifice" with the ulterior motive and incentive of some payback or reward. Through a mutual challenge, the very interaction constitutes its own satisfaction. One does not expect "sweet words", "nice gifts" or signs of gratitude, although they will be welcome whenever they come, and they probably will come naturally, without any immediate necessity or pressure. Since an OI is conscious of his own existential struggle, knowing existence is a permanent challenge, he will be conscious of this issue in his love partner, thus he will be attentive and caring about this issue.

Love dominates, love submits, love does not care much about domination or submission. Love uses, love is used, but love hardly cares about using or being used. It fears neither power nor utility. It is not very respectful, it is too passionate for that. It neither fears, nor loathes, nor adores neither pain nor pleasure. To the extent its object is worth all the sacrifices, all the dedication. As the demon of Nieztsche claims, with its promise or threat of eternal recurrence: 'This life as you now live it and have lived it, you will have to live once more and innumerable times more; and there will be nothing new in it, but every pain and every joy and every thought and sigh and everything unutterably small or great in your life will have to return to you, all in the same succession and sequence".

Nevertheless, one interesting phenomenon is that such an attitude is in a way extended to any human being, whoever he is, whatever the nature of the relation, although probably less intensively. Thus the demarcation between relatives and others will not be so strongly established. Such a solid opposition is grounded in a primitive worldview where humans are competing for "finite goods", where the interest of one is determined in opposition to the interest of the others. The close people then become the ones with whom we have a mutual pact of protection, with them we possess and protect some good, against the "others", the outsiders that threaten us.

In this sense we can say that an OI relation is noticeable through the characteristics that it is open to the world, instead of a "mafia" type of dynamic where the interest of the close ones is privileged and protected through a latent or open conflict with non-intimate people. Such a view, in which many children are educated, provides a very limited and reductionist horizon and worldview, actually a very base and lowly self-conception. Thus this romantic or sentimental worldview of relations extends very naturally to the close circle of family members, including some friends or allies, in a pact of self-protection: us against them. Although such alliances often remain fragile, superficial and unstable, modifying over time, depending on the vagaries of circumstances, in opposition to the relative stability of the OI scheme. In such a perspective, we are supposed to be complacent with family members and harsh with the outsiders. We criticize and punish the "others", we are more tolerating and accepting with "ours". Although such a principle is rather illusory, because this "pleasant" internal attitude will always face the reality principle that each member of the family has as well his own self-interest, that will be different or opposed to the interest of the community or individual interest of other members of the group. And if the members of the group are not trained and ready to deal in a rational and meaningful way to whoever they intimately relate to, thus the restricted group, like often in families, becomes in time a battlefield, where the "enemy" is just as well inside, maybe even worse.

Bonding

An interesting feature of the sentimental or romantic family and relational attitude, is the concept of "bonding". Bonding designates the formation and establishment of a close relationship, like between mother and child or even between a person and an animal, especially through frequent or constant association and interaction. It can be a close friendship developing between adults, for example as a result of intense common experiences. It is the process by which an intense emotional or sentimental relation is developed, but as well it is the expression of such relation and the result of this process. But bonding in itself does not necessitate any substantial content, it can simply express and nurture some purely sentimental attachment. Bonding dialogues, like chit-chat and childish games between lovers, can seem totally meaningless and ridiculous to the external observer, although from the inside it is felt as cute, charming or moving.

Through the bonding process, one feels united, connected, related to someone else, which means to be less lonely and isolated. Of course, one can bond with some meaningful content, sharing ideas, activity and experiences. But in the "romantic" relation, the bonding often ignores any content; it is beyond content, it is even deprived of any content: it is its own content. Basic and popular bonding is quite undemanding, it is fed by trivia, it can even be proud of being trivialized, of not requesting any real content, thus manifesting its freedom, power and beauty. "True lovers" bond with absolutely anything, since they are "deeply" in love. And because of this, there is a trivialization of the self. Trivia are unimportant matters, details or information that furnish a good part of daily conversation, verbal exchanges that are designated as "small talk". This recourse to trivia indicates nothing more than the complacent blandness and vapidity of human behavior, a regrettable but common pattern, although some claim it facilitates daily exchanges. But the romantic behavior goes further, by attributing, most likely unconsciously, some value to this trivia, from which the qualification of imposture. Just because this trivia is exchanged between the two lovers, it is endowed with a dimension of wonder, greatness, transcendence, beauty, fascination, etc., of course inaccessible to common mortals. If those trivia are opinions, they will be true and unquestionable, since what constitutes the substance of the love exchange, no matter how superficial, unreflected and idotic it is, cannot be false or doubtful, since it emerges from and is carried by a sublime process or wonderful state. So it is in the family culture, since those little things or references are privy to an "our people"identity, some exclusive and of course great belonging, it symbolizes our special, homy and implicitly "better"way of being, compared to the neighbors. Like we said, the content is irrelevant to bonding, it avoids any critical thinking, but worse, it actually hinders any real content by glorifying trivia. And in this process the subject is trivialized, reduced to nonsense, while being satisfied with it. Or the interaction is reduced to exchanging primitive needs. And this satisfaction is circumstantial, since it is based on the recognition of a minute group of people; anyone else, the majority of people or common sense would find it brainless and empty. Its value has no universality, its worthiness or interest is merely based on an occasional connivance, through some tacit and arbitrary agreement. The meaning of the bonding is very private, and in a way we can grant it some private value, a sentimental price, like some cheap trinket that has value uniquely because it comes from our ancestors.This would not be a problem if this phenomenon did not dilute or drown any thinking or annihilate any minimal sense of reality, if we did not forget the desultory meaning or significance of those "trinkets", and if we did not favor those trifles, which slowly replace anything more significant and challenging, inducing a strong form of collective complacency. Until the day one of the players in the romantic or family relationship, for some reason rebels, refusing to play anymore the game of inanity or consensus. Such a rupture is generally experienced as a betrayal, which rarely happens without some passion and violence.

Thus those lovers speak about nothing, they are charmed by the pronunciation of mere words, as sugary as possible, far from any challenge that would nourish their relationship in the long term. But through time, as the varnish wears off, either they move on to something more substantial, or various problems will set in when one of them starts seeing the real person in front of him, slowly getting bored or even disgusted with the sweet idiocy. But for some strange reason, some persons persist in this glorification of the other or the group, their only access to transcendence, developing therefore a powerful strain of dependency, rarely requited, at least not to the extent expected, which generates a form of resentment. A typical traditional discrepancy in the couple is the wife who pretends to make out of her husband the alpha and omega of her existence, while he views his wife as a mere predicate of his existence. Or the parents that overinvest the relation to their children, while those, even if they appreciate their parents, or not at all, are more concerned with leading their own autonomous existence.

In bonding, intention is primary, and there is no relation of necessity between the content of the message and its intention. The message must simply provoke nice feelings in an aleatory way, by using little things evoking some intimacy. One must say stupid things that he would never say to anyone else without feeling ashamed of his own stupidity. The reason is that in a romantic or familial relation we presuppose a full unconditional acceptance of the self. And it is obvious that such a "full acceptance" cannot last, for example it is possible only in the drunkenness of some initial moment of "crush". The literal definition of the verb "to crush" is here interesting: to compress or squeeze forcefully so as to break, damage, or distort in shape. In those moments, we indeed are not ourselves, our reason is distorted: our thinking guard is down, an attitude which conditions the "full acceptance". We don't need to check what we say, quality of speech does not matter, each one becomes the garbage bin of the other. There is no demand, no critical thinking, no need of understanding, all we care about is the connection. We don't want content, the other person becomes an end in itself, not the means for some thinking or accomplishment, exactly the reverse of an OI relation. The transcendence stops with the person, we can actually own it since the person is mine, and I am transcendence by belonging to him. Indeed, to be loved does produce a strange state of mind, where one becomes a sort of God. But in reality, this transcendent other which is supposed to be "all", is actually an imposture, since he is the embodiment of a circumstance. Indeed he has a special status. But this status is fragile, it depends on the moods, on time, on the instability of the world, it is a contrived unconditional. In fact, our existence rests upon the weakness and inconsistency of another miserable subject, the main reason why lovers are so moody, irritable and anxious.

Love engenders a false sense of transcendence since the loved one actually saturates the space and horizon of his lover. Of course, we don't speak here about a wider conception of love, like love for a nation, an ideal or humanity, a passion which provides a totally different setting, a quite legitimate access to transcendence. In an individual relation, lovers often don't share a goal, they are each other as a goal, attempting an impossible fusion. We should specify in this context that to bring forth children is not so much a goal but more of a consequence.

Love for a single person cannot constitute an existential goal, at least not in a primary function. Unless they already share a common goal, outside of themselves. This is the case for two main reasons. First, because the opening to the world is clogged up by the object of adoration, rather reduced, prohibiting any wider perspective. Second, because such a relation cannot be a purpose in itself regulating in a meaningful way one's overall activity. We can here evoke the life of those wives who have nothing else to worry about than their husband, who become bored and rather desperate, unless they find for themselves some other goal or activity. Therefore the love relation can only play a secondary although important role, to the extent it breathes and allows breathing, instead of being a vector for asphyxia. It is in itself too grounded, bound to a limited field, a singular person, it cannot constitute a decent transcendent regulatory ideal. In order to open to transcendance, the loved one should be an icon, not an idol, he should be a passage, not a dead end, he should be a path, not a destination. The idol is adored in itself, it is loved and admired as a self-contained object. The icon is a mere reflection, it symbolizes, recalls, indicates, manifests something greater than itself. The idol is empirical, its existence is a given, it "is"; the icon is transcendent, its existence is a call toward something greater than itself, it points towards being, it is not "being". In the first case, love invites the subject to certitude and complacency; in the second, love is an aspiration, an act of defiance of the self. Too often, the love relation resumes itself, as an ideal, to the mutual satisfaction of two empirical selves. It constitutes a warrior's resting place, and not the preparation for a worthy battle. And in reality, this satisfaction is quite egocentric, a phenomenon that is revealed when one does not obtain anymore what he wants and then in return is not motivated to satisfy the needs of the partner, the main reason for a breakup.

In the love phenomenon, we often encounter a desire to be loved unconditionally, to be loved absolutely. In such a perspective, the object which the "other" must make me be is an object of transcendence, an absolute center of reference around which all the instrumental things of the world are ordered as pure means, a love for which any quality, action or predicate is secondary. I am not loved "because", I am loved "in spite of", I am loved just for myself. The only acceptable "because" is "because I am who I am". I am considered as the absolute limit of such love, as the absolute source of all values, as a limit of the other's freedom, I am a priori therefore protected against any eventual devalorization. I am the absolute value. And to the extent that I assume my being-for-others, I assume myself as value in itself. Thus to want to be loved is to want to be placed beyond the whole system of values posited by the other, to be the condition of all valorization and the objective foundation of all values. If the other loves me, then I become the unsurpassable, which means that I must be the absolute end. In this sense I am saved from any instrumentalization. My existence in the midst of such a world becomes the exact correlate of my transcendence-for-myself since my autonomy and self-value is absolutely safe guarded. In such a scheme, the lover, being loved, wants to be "the whole world" for the beloved. This means that he puts himself aside from the world, since he is the one who assumes and symbolizes the world. In a paradoxical way, he consents to be an object. But he wants to be the object in which the other's freedom desires to lose itself, the object in which the other accepts to find and limit his being and his raison d'être.

"All I have in my life is you" says the lover to his beloved, or the parent to his child, a very common and popular statement. As if the other person was his only reason for living, a sad prospect. First, it is about possession, since we use the verb "to have". Second, our life has no meaning outside of our loved one, a quite pathetic form of self-denigration, denying the richness of one's life. Third, the pressure that is put on that other can be quite unbearable for him, who is told that the existence of a third person rests entirely on his own shoulders. Very often, without even asking his opinion. We find this as well in the classical parental statement: "Everything I do, I do it for you". Fourth, it is a quite narrow-minded worldview, with a focus on a very tiny part of reality, ignoring the globality of the world, disregarding all the other people. Fifth, it is a very anxiogenic scheme, where the slightest action or word of this other person, their presence or absence, determines our fate, our happiness or misfortune, the meaning of our life. And anyway such a statement can only be false and illusory. However, this existence by proxy is often bathed in a romantic halo, since only this beloved other counts, a speech or an attitude that too easily forgets that it is also the sign of capitulation, even of complacency. Since I have you, I no longer need to question myself and my existence, any more than I need to question your existence: your mere presence suffices to fill all my expectations, a fictitious scheme if there is one. This "other" then becomes the artificial lung through which we breathe, without which we pretend to die.

"Love is infinity within reach of poodles", wrote Céline. It offers a feeling of eternity for cheap. Love is an accomplishment, not the condition for a relationship. Otherwise it is a consumer product. Too often, the other, the object of our desire, becomes a false transcendence, a decoy, in the sense that it becomes an idol, a finite god, a fixed entity, and therefore with time a decaying corpse. And in this adulterated manner the imposture of being is one of circumstance, tied up to possession, to being possessed, to complacently satisfying needs and to being rewarded for it. Real love occurs, can occur, when one is available to actual transcendence, to mutual transcendence, transcendence of self, transcendence of the other, the very condition for a relationship worthy of the name. Accompanying each other with each one's endeavor, which each one's sense of a radical ontological shortcoming. Without pathetic pity nor miserable condescension. Challenge, instead of fear, accompaniment instead of control, an infinite perspective, the vanishing and undetermined condition that may define the only possibility of an actual fusion, since one remains conscious of the discrepancy of human existence, within oneself, within the bond. Trust replaces fear, since the loss becomes impossible: it makes no sense, its impossibility deriving from the absence of possession. The other is a separate being, our own self is a separate being, a strange object to its own consciousness. Comfort remains the enemy. Any sensible initiative goes against self-interest, and maintains the other in a state of permanent surprise. Detachment, and detachment of the detachment. The other, the object of our admiration, is great out of not being great, out of embodying his not-greatness, shamelessly, without any pretension nor feeling of self-sacrifice. Unconditional love is possible, since there are no expectations, since each one remains himself and allows the other one to struggle with himself, without pity nor condescension. Possession and complacency, the static instinct of comfort, in other words the desire to control, must be put to sleep, by recognizing the weakness of its essence, the insubstantiality of its power. The other estranges himself from his own self, we feel like we cannot recognize him anymore, he is abandoning us, but we tag along, eager to discover the other side of this Rubicon. What pitiful criticism is the one that claims: "You have changed! I don't recognize you anymore!". Of course, he is not mine, he does not have to pay dues, he simply has to pursue his own course. He should not care that we want to feel satiated, that we hope to feel replete and dulled. Self-challenge, other-challenge, are totally synonymous and congruent. Otherwise the complicity becomes one of imposture, the vain contentment of trivia, the commodification of being. Comfort is thought of as an alternative to struggle, but it is actually the sign of a most sordid defeat.

The love reduction

The way people love probably reveals who they are more than anything else, since it is the very immediate expression of their being. And it is too often the expression of an infantile self. First they are mesmerized, one is willing to sacrifice anything to the fusional experience, since the other one is such a wonderful being, and it is so extraordinary to be loved by him. But gloss and excitement wear out with time, through repetition and permanent interaction with the real person. One realizes that this amazing being is just a normal human being, more real and less fascinating. Thus the lover gets worn out and tired, he starts to have needs. Sacrifice disappears from the order of things, and the "lover" expects his needs to be satisfied. This is the moment when the other can be the cause of disappointment, since the payback is often not up to par. Each one calculates, evaluates the yield and return of the arrangement. Often a frustrating evaluation, especially in comparison with the ecstasy of the initial moment. In this primitive description, although rather common, we are far from the experience of love as an adventure of mutual challenge and common accomplishment.

Lovers love to bond and share, they rejoice about the idea that they can see and show each other the most minute folds of their souls, they entertain a deep sense of intimacy, a very romantic sensation. They even have the impression of partaking in a common soul, undergoing the same thoughts, the same impressions, the same emotions. Thus having no secret one for the other, a very enthralling perspective. But rather quickly, they have to realize the impossibility of such an ideal, if only because the "other" is so sensitive, so fragile, and we don't want to hurt his feelings, we don't want to cause him pain, a sensitivity that prohibits frankness and authenticity. And as time goes by, more and more, an apprenticeship generally punctuated by diverse incidents or quarrels, the lover discovers he cannot say anymore what he thinks: certain subjects have to be avoided, certain sensitive observations or criticisms have to be definitely hushed, certain taboos are put into place, certain issues have to never be mentioned. That is where the challenge stops, where is put into place an anxiogenic zone of comfort as a condition for the continuation of the relationship. "Do not tell me, even if it is obvious!", is the password for such an arrangement.

Slowly, in the love relation, the need to seduce and charm the other one, hiding our worst character traits, is replaced by a feeling of a certain indebtedness: we are owed something. The other now has to satisfy us, be attentive to our needs, he should not make us upset, he should not demand too much: he should give us what we expect. After the sweet initial desire to please and to share, comes the harsh demands: "having rights" and "demanding respect". The focus is not anymore on the needs of another person, but on our own. There comes the fundamental separation, when "love relation" becomes a "business plan", the home of disenchantment. Bonding becomes suffocating, too overwhelming, and a person goes back to being a subject that has to be treated in a certain way, carefully, actually becoming a consumer. And individual existence takes over togetherness. The debt becomes an object of calculation: I have spent so many years, I have sacrificed so much, I have given "everything", but now has come payback time, long overdue. Enough is enough, I have sufficiently been a patsy, forced into a raw deal. Resentment is hidden in terms like justice, equality, fairness, since I have been cheated all this time, since I have been abused through my ingenuity. I have sacrificed myself beyond reasonable boundaries, the limit has been reached, the bill now has to be footed. Of course, there might be some legitimacy to such a speech, like all discourses it has reasons to be, some grounding in reality. Thus the thirst for equality can change society, it is at the origin of many reforms and revolutions. The main problem is that one forgets too easily that if he accepted such a raw deal, he must have received some satisfaction and benefit from it: to be a victim is a comfortable position. But the soul gets tired in time, it lacks energy, and the focus shifts toward the other as a "bad provider", the lover becomes the victim of the one who imposed this terrible scheme for his own abusive benefit. From which the anger and the resentment, the powerful sense of victimhood. Nietzsche has an interesting comment about this idea of sacrifice: "If we make sacrifices in doing good or in doing ill, it does not alter the ultimate value of our actions; even if we stake our life in the cause, as martyrs do for the sake of our church: it is a sacrifice to our longing for power, or for the purpose of conserving our sense of power." Although he suspects that the problem was already there since the beginning. "But that which the all-too-many, the superfluous, call marriage—alas, what shall I name that? Alas, this poverty of the soul in pair! Alas, this filth of the soul in pair! Alas, this wretched contentment in pair! Marriage they call this." Here, we could make a vicious pun, by saying that behind the pair hides despair. We could echo the platonic myth of the split being: we are looking for another being because of the deep sense of inadequacy of our self; something is missing, we need some other entity that will provide us with a sense of completeness. Of course, at first we feel fulfilled, like when hungry we are provided with a hefty meal. To discover later on that no meal can ever protect us from an eternal sense of hunger, our satisfaction will always be superficial and temporary. Thus, either we accept this sense of finitude and the anguish that accompanies it, or we start despising a world that cannot provide us with our lawful need for completion. How then can we not be disappointed with this miserable other using us for his own needs, ignoring the torments of our own soul. We have strong feelings about the whole issue, from the beginning until the end, no matter the nature of those diverse and opposite feelings. But instead of taking those feelings with distance, prudence and circumspection, we rush to protect them, to nurture them, to believe them, to justify them, we brood them like our most precious belongings. Furthermore, a couple is like a sounding board, a device that increases and amplifies the sound produced by the individual souls. Thus we have the choice. Either our individual existence is one of challenge and access to some ideal, responding to some transcendent call, thus the couple becomes an empowering entity. Or our existence is one of primitive needs and a quest for petty comfort, thus the romantic initial impulse will quickly turn into some self-destructive maelstrom, or more peacefully it will become the practical arrangement of two business partners.

After the initial moment of excitement is gone, some couples get preoccupied with "rekindling the passion", wanting to bring back the intensity of the original feeling of being in love. This feeling was for them the access to transcendence, as through the romantic intensity one was granted some meaning, one's being was glorified and so was the being of another person. They want to relive that excitement. Through being an object for the other, one became a real subject, a center of attention, an important point of focus, since he is "the whole world" for someone else. One then has an impression of being a gate to transcendence for someone else, an intoxicating arousal, that is why they can agree to being a tool for another person, to be used or even abused, as long as they are needed, as long as through the other they can overexist. Sartre called this state "masochism", a sweetened sense of failure, surrendering to another person, giving him the power to overrule us, and through this devaluation of the self, come to be. In this sense any intense feeling of love is a mixture of subjective masochism and deification: one both disappears and is transcended.

But after some time, or periodically, the intensity diminishes and one slowly comes back to oneself, to one's finiteness, to being one's own end. Some disillusion takes place, through habit, routine or irritation, what was fascinating at first can become bothersome, by coming into close contact, the otherness can seem too "other". There can as well be some unevenness of investment: while one is too involved, another person can be more distant, or one can simply worry too much about one's status in the eyes of a partner. Moreover nothing can remain in the same state eternally, so it is bound to take another shape. But unlike the initial ecstatic moment, this later state carries a weight of finiteness, there is no more fusion and if one is not reconciled with oneself, this stage will be full of dissatisfaction, anxieties and pains. One is back to feeling like an impostor: I am no more the world for someone else, I am again a derelict, a wanderer, not fundamentally needed nor wanted. That is why for some to envisage a rupture is a terrible prospect, it signifies a passage from being "someone" to being "no one". So the passion has to be rekindled, so that one can have a guarantee of existence, no matter the fragility of this guarantee.

We as well observe another dynamic in long term love relations, just as in family relations: the petty fighting, about everything and nothing. A usual and recurrent process of bickering, light or intense, depending on the personality and the culture of the protagonists, on the context and the nature of the relation. It emotionally ranges from passive aggressive pouting to actual physical confrontation. It plays a cathartic effect, since it allows the expression of our existential frustration, of our disappointment with oneself and with the other. It maintains a certain liveliness in the relationship, in order to avoid the boredom of purely businesslike exchanges, although the practical aspect constitutes the main reality of the situation. And since happiness is often a backlash of unhappiness, those painful disputes and fits of anger pleasantly provide the opportunity of moving apologies and joyful reconciliations. Some couples are for example very addicted to the "fight and fuck" system, a quite erotic stratagem for the enthusiast. As if anger was a necessary component of the love relation.

Of course, one can always defend arguing as an inevitable component of human relation, especially when people permanently share the same life space, when they build their life together, when they develop intimacy. In order to foster trust, one should not remain permanently silent about what preoccupies him or what bothers him in the other person. One has to listen, one has to speak, the emotional dimension of such exchanges cannot and should not be avoided. In spite of their mutual attachment, partners in a relationship still have their own personal interest and specific agenda, a difference that will engender conflict and arguing. Honesty can strengthen intimacy, since through conflicts one gets to know and understand better the other, just like it can nourish antagonism, which is the reason why silence will or will not be a privileged strategy, depending on the situation. Some prefer the silence of submission, allowing abuse, others prefer the silence of sulking, expressing frustration, but both silence lead to unhappiness and resentment. Sulking is that terrible, infantile and violent practice, a mortal silence forbidding itself of any words, any explanations, with the following rationality: "If he really loved me, he should know". Unless the silence simply signifies that the game is not worth the candle anymore, the sign of a purely practical arrangement, an emotional disengagement. But when the fighting is frequent and repetitive, when it is mainly concerned with petty issues, when reason does not tend to prevail and fights cease only out of exhaustion, when anger is regularly a strong component, we can see it is a sign of stagnation and decay in the relationship.

In terms of the scheme of the imposture, if the conflict remains tempered, when it remains the sign of a mutual existential commitment, when it authorizes rationality, it belongs to the ontological imposture, since one remains aware of the work to be done, in relation to oneself and in relation to the interaction. The friction with the other remains the opportunity to get to know oneself better and to learn decentering, which remains a meaningful and satisfying accomplishment that love feeds upon. If the friction with the other becomes systematic and latent, if it constantly tends to end with a feeling of bitterness and incomprehension, if it does not bring anything fundamental on the existential level, then it belongs to the circumstantial imposture. The other is there to make up for our own shortcomings, to satisfy our needs, to conceal our real existential problems, using him as the scapegoat of our own helplessness, as the outlet for our own frustration. Love here becomes an illusory term, it is only the illicit name for a fear of emptiness and loneliness, or the clinging to a habit.

Simone Weil in Waiting for God, writing about friendship or love, describes how the feeling deteriorates when it falls into the order of need: need for services, need for reassurance, need for companionship, etc. What was initially of the order of the search for the good degrades into need, like a drug. "When the attachment of one human being to another is constituted by need alone, it is an atrocious thing. Few things in the world can reach this degree of ugliness and horror... The human soul possesses, it is true, a whole arsenal of lies to protect itself against this ugliness and to fabricate in imagination false good where there is only necessity."

Once one can engage in a noble fight, he does not fear breaching the pact of comfort and convenience, when such a decision seems to impose itself. Be it out of one's existential necessity or out of such a necessity for the other. Although in order to commit such a crucial and decisive action, one has to learn to pick his battles. When daily life is exhausted by petty bickering, no space and energy is left for such an important decisive endeavor. If a person is constantly engaged in the satisfaction of his immediate needs, he will not have the audacity and clarity of mind allowing such commitment to infringe the status quo and the implicit agreement. But happiness is actually too often considered a private matter. At best the other is thought about as satisfying my needs, not as a challenge for himself, even less for society as a whole. Nevertheless, strangely enough, after the critical lines we wrote about the exhilaration of romantic love, let us state that the incapacity to undergo such an emotional experience at some point in our life, intense and brief, would seem to be a form of psychological handicap. Falling in love is a constitutive dimension of the human psyche, although its drunkenness can become quite addictive and illusory. One simply has to learn how to drink and consume in a mature way, it needs reason, restrain and self-control, that is why alcohol is forbidden for children.

The romantic aesthetics

Let us add in a more general way that another form of romantic imposture is brought into being in a certain worldview, what can loosely be called romanticism, the romantic aesthetics, where the glorification of feelings takes over when our existence is in itself not so satisfying. Thus we look for drama that makes us vibrate, no matter the content of this drama, the "soap opera" principle, favoring sentimentality, in particular such feelings as pity or enthrallment. Nostalgia is as well popular, when we fabricate a myth with our past, a combination of objective memories and embellishment in various proportions. Or nature, in its pacific unchangeable eternal modality, for example a forest, in its violent and dramatic modality, such as volcanoes, storms, torrents, or in its animality, wild or domestic, savage or friendly but always touching. In all these cases, we attribute to our contemplation a capacity to take us out of this boring or horrible world, we indeed attribute to it some transcendent quality, but it engages us in a rather passive behavior, without much challenge. We admire this reality, we relate to it, it engenders emotions or peace, but it does not allow us to confront our own self. Thus we remain a circumstantial impostor, bound to some environment, a feature that does not fundamentally change our daily life, beside offering some type of temporary consolation. In the romantic imposture, we long for drama and sentimentality that will make us vibrate, that will allow us to momentarily overexist by taking us out of this boring and tedious world. Some people have one fear in mind: that of failing their life. Absurd concept if there is one. No doubt they prevent themselves from living by wanting to live, by hoping or by pretending in reality to overexist. The happiness of some obscure and vague satisfaction, intense and eternal. This may be explained by the fact that our fellow citizens generally spend several hours a day in front of their television set, Netflix, or some other purveyor of dreams and fantasies. As a part of his drunkenness scheme, the CI has a need for the wonderful and the hyperbolic: great weekend, idyllic environment, marvelous time, wonderful family, fantastic holidays, etc.

Furthermore, the romantic imposture, as we see in romantic art, fabricates a pseudo reality, an augmented or distorted reality, that we use in order to escape the dullness and hardship of this present or immediate reality. The romantic drive is an attempt to make reality fit our feelings, it is supposed to satisfy our emotional perceptions: we want to be pleased, to be enthused, to be excited, to be ecstatic. It attempts to create a sense of immediate fulfillment and achievement, we can actually reach and touch the ultimate, the unconditional, the absolute. Absorbed in the contemplation of this fascinating object we have fabricated, obsessed with the altar we have erected and that we idolize, we do not need to go further: we have reached the end, an end that is sublimated in some form of transcendence. Of course, this romantic drive plays a function in the human mind, and there is no reason why we should not benefit from the pleasure it provides. Why not enjoy the state of drunkenness provided by a work of art, by a song, by nature, by a form or another of beauty! But if such an impulse incites the artist to further its creation, permanently seeking new accomplishments, it becomes obvious complacency when it becomes a mere act of consumption, when it does not lead someone to some type of accomplishment.

However, what applies to the consumer also resonates with the artist. Let's take a look at the situation. An artist embarks on his work. He incorporates his intuition, he articulates his idea and materializes it. He forgets himself in its implementation. It is both an affirmation of oneself and a negation of oneself, through an actualization of the transcendent subject. The problem arises when this work is used as the production of an inebriation that cannot last, the romantic moment. Because the artist cannot always and continuously create, he always ends up falling back on himself, finding himself again, he cannot ignore himself eternally. And when he is forced to think and be conscious, he is obliged to consider the discrepancy between his existence and his ideal, as well as the pain of his unfulfilled expectations, the weight of his empirical and circumstantial needs that seem to demean him in his own eyes. He therefore fears of no longer existing, of discovering his own inner gap, his state of "almost nothing", of "less than nothing". After the ecstasy of the work, the depression of existence. There he has a choice: to confront himself, or to try to escape the principle of reality, necessarily paying the psychological cost of such betrayal. Unfortunately, too often, what drives him to work, what motivates him, is articulated precisely through this effort of escape. Therein lies the principle of the tragic artist, even the doomed artist. And what we have just described for the artist also applies to any person engaged in an intense activity, in a passion, whether he is an intellectual, a businessman, an activist, an association manager, as long as there is a significant existential investment in this activity. Of course, the emotional tone and psychological positioning can vary depending on the nature of the activity. But one always ends up nonetheless falling back on the finitude and the flatness of the self.

The artist faces emptiness: he does not know what will land on the paper or the canvas. He leaps towards the unknown. When the forms finally appear, when they slowly take shape, he can exclaim "I know it! I knew it all along! I recognize myself!" He can then wonder where the doubt came from, what was this idea that he could not paint anymore. He was disenchanted, he had lost courage, he felt the weight of inertia, he was abandoned by the expected state of bliss, but now it comes back to him, once he crossed the wall of fire or uncertainty and he took the risk of dirtying up the blank slate. Those moments are tragic, when he feels paralyzed, when he cannot do anything anymore. But if he chooses to truly and fully be an artist, he can live peacefully these empty passages: he accepts his destiny, permanently awaiting inspiration, or bypassing the illusion of such a concept. His inertia, his depression, his abandon and anxiety are grounded in a desire of "elsewhere", a thirst for some ultramundane harmonious reality, it is caused by the painful return to a raspy, flat or strident earth, and it provokes such a depressive mental state. Circumstantial imposture. This passion for an elsewhere which can never be attained nor discovered makes the artist a permanent exile, ostracized from a promised paradise, forever suffering and damned. At the same time, this confrontation of the self, its resistance, its accomplishment, are nourished by this belief in an impossible elsewhere, something infinitely greater than his poor self. And unfortunately, in some brief moments, he seems to slightly touch this eden, an ephemeral rapture that reinforces in his soul the conviction there is such a possibility, there is such an accessible reality.

Chekov, a great analyst of the human psyche, vividly and perspicaciously describes the romantic imposture, for example in "The Three Sisters". The play spans several years in the Prozorov siblings' lives, during which each of them pines for a future that seems unattainable: a return to their beloved hometown of Moscow, which through nostalgia represents an escape from a mediocre life and all the unattainable things they desire. By showing his characters entangling themselves in reminiscence and pining, Chekov argues that as long as people are fixated on what they do not have, happiness will be constantly beyond their reach. Olga reminisces about leaving Moscow years ago: "I remember very well, at the beginning of May like now, in Moscow everything is already in bloom, it is warm, everything is bathed in sunshine", since the present merely rekindles this yearning: "This morning I woke up, I saw a mass of light, I saw the spring, joy welled up in my soul and I had a huge longing for home." Many years later, Moscow is still "home" to Olga, and any beauty in her provincial residence leads not to the contentment of where she is, but a melancholy desire for a better "elsewhere". Of course, the plans to move back to Moscow never come to fruition. Irina despises her "boring" life: "What I wanted, what I dreamed of, it definitely does not have." Thus she obsesses over the "lost land": "I dream of Moscow every night. I'm just like a madwoman" . She believes that moving there is the only way to fulfill all her suppressed desires. Masha even claims that if she was in Moscow, she would not mind the poor weather. A more realist character, Vershinin, argues that happiness doesn't really exist, only the desire for it is real. "We have no happiness, and it doesn't exist, we only desire it."

In fact, living in Moscow would not really fulfill the sisters' longings: when obtaining the object of their desire, they would most likely transfer their longings elsewhere. Irina claims that "If we were going to move to Moscow, I would meet my true love, I dreamed of him, I loved him." Although she admits as well that "All that turned out to be nonsense." But still, she exclaims: "Only let us go to Moscow! I beg you, let us go! There is nothing better than Moscow in the whole world!" Moscow has become a symbol of contentment in her mind, more than a real place. Their brother Andrey confesses: "Every night I dream that I am a professor at Moscow University, a famous scholar who is Russia's pride!" But consciousness periodically surges, his rant is quickly followed by agitation and weeping, and he tells the women, "My darling sisters [···] do not believe me, do not believe me···" No matter how Andrey tries to portray his situation, his unhappiness is not far beneath the surface. He clings to the hope of some vague prospect: "The present is repulsive, but when I think of the future how wonderful things become! There's a feeling of ease, of space, in the distance there's a glimmer of the dawn, I see freedom, I see myself and my children freed from idleness, from the ignoble life." Like his sisters, Andrey longs for a more engaging life than that of provincial leisure and conventionality; but it is just a "glimmer," with no more substance than the sisters' dreams of Moscow. Strikingly, by the end of the play, the only character who seems to find real happiness is the elderly servant Anfisa who, when given a lodging and nourishment, marvels, "A big apartment, nothing to pay, and I have a little room all to myself and a bed. All free. I wake up at night, and O Lord, Mother of God, there is no human being happier than me!"This ending supports Chekov's argument that gratitude is the key to contentment, gratitude for whatever is already granted to us, joyfully accepting the present, or reconciling with it. Longing for the past or for the future is a way to avoid the immediate, to avoid dealing with the finiteness of reality and to live in the imposture of a mere phantasmatic possible, be it the complacency of nostalgia or wonderful expectations. A speaking example of illusory transcendence.

In order to conclude our analysis of the romantic imposture, let us summarize the main reasons why, in spite of its own function and legitimacy, romanticism can represent a problem and how it can foster imposture. First, one focuses on his mere feelings, a very private, reduced and not reflexive attitude that prohibits or warps access to reality, engendering a quite illusory perception, deprived of reason and critical thinking. Second, it induces a rather passive state, rendering one rather impotent, weak and inactive, by inducing a mere contemplative behavior, even objectifying oneself. Third, it magnifies and glorifies its object, a process of hyperbolization in which the individual can drown himself, losing ground and balance, disconnecting from reality. By the same token, it can have a similar effect on the other person when this person is the object of the romantic impulse. Fourth, one can become complacent, both in relation to his own being and in relation to the object of his admiration, giving up on any substantial challenge of himself and "other", since one feels replete with the "ownership" of his object. Fifth, romanticism is quick burning, the intensity and hyperbole is difficult to sustain over the long term, the flame is always condemned to fading and extinction, therefore the subject will undergo a permanent manic-depressive state, quite unstable and painful, rather addictive. Therefore we can conclude from this that any fundamental ontological perspective will be lost, the horizon being occupied by some glamorized and venerated concrete object, saturating the mental space of the subject, providing him with a vain sense of satisfaction, ephemeral and insubstantial.

Passions and feelings   Often, passions are distinguished from feelings by comparing their strength, their intensity or their depth, a rather quantitative determination where passions seem to have "more" than feelings, for both are equally defined as "affective states". But it seems that there are some further specific characteristics that would establish their difference, partially as a consequence of this "more". We will exclude emotions from this comparison, since they are rather momentary psychological phenomena, when feelings and passions are more characteristic of a continuous process. Emotions are a particular moment of intense feeling, often accompanied by visible physiological manifestations, which cannot maintain themselves for a long time due to their intensity, although they can be reactivated periodically. We will propose different differences or oppositions between passion and feelings, although those distinctions are not always so clear cut and can overlap.

Active - Passive   Feelings tend to be passive and contemplative, when passion generally leads to some type of action, be it passion for someone or for some activity. Undergoing passion makes people more daring and outspoken when feelings can be quite secretive and quiescent. Both can be overwhelming, the former by producing action, the latter by impeding it. Generally, passion engenders or produces something, be it some objects, events or processes. It is so powerful that it has to externalize itself. Feelings remain rather unseen, or perceived by a small number of people, and open onto very limited actions if any. Even the passion for a person invites us to some action, if only to please, seduce or impress this person.

Outward - Inward Passion transcends the individual, when feelings are more cententered on his subjectivity. In this sense, passion englobes a larger scale and perspective; it is outer-directed. Passion leads the subject toward the outside, when feelings make him focus on himself, it is inner-directed.

Collective - Particular Feelings are restrained to oneself, at best they are shareable with a small number of people, but their vocation is not particularly to be communicated to all. We can express our feelings in order to be heard, but often a passionate person wants others to undergo a similar process and it can even have a universal pretension, especially the passion for an ideal.

Means - End In passion, a subject is the means to something greater than him, some ideal or transcendence, while with feelings, the enjoyment –or pain –of the perception is the end, something we undergo in itself. Unless of course we make it an object of reflection, but then it is not feeling anymore. Feelings are generally not meant as a path to overcome the subject. Passion can live even after a particular subject is gone, transmitted to other persons, or its object can survive.

Indifference - Pleasure and pain A subject that is focused on feelings generally wants to be pleased, he wants his feelings to be soothed, taken into consideration, respected, etc., and he wants his unpleasant feelings to disappear, since they make him unhappy. A passionate subject can withstand unpleasant feelings, such as pain, disappointment, frustration, etc., since his fundamental issue is beyond feelings. Passion is a strong factor of resilience, it helps to endure the vagaries of life. The passionate will of course welcome pleasant feelings, while not being attached to them, since they are not his main purpose. His satisfaction is largely connected to some accomplishment, something outside of himself.

Persistent - Ephemeral   Passion maintains itself through time and space, rather indifferent to circumstances. External events generally cannot eradicate it or modify it. Feelings are very susceptible to the environment, they adjust according to events, they are more plastic than passion. That is why "feeling people" are moody, their state of mind varies often in an unpredictable way. When passion installs itself more as an existential anchoring. It is rather obsessive, it primarily doesn't want to know anything but itself, it becomes a need, it has a continuous nature. Feelings are more fleeting and superficial, they don't constitute a primary existential motivation, it has a rather discontinuous nature.

Challenge - Complacency   Passion implies the relation to some type of transcendence or absolute that demands a permanent effort on the part of the subject, in an endless way, since its goal can never be completely accomplished or exhausted. Its being is permanently undergoing some tension. The feeling subject on the other side contemplates his own feeling, be it pleasurable or painful, enjoying it or suffering from it, a state which does not imply any further action or challenge. He maintains himself in his psychological state, unconsciously glorifying it as a reality in itself, unsurpassable, as if it were eternal. It will only be modified by external events or by the arbitrariness of some uncontrollable internal process. The subject remains uncritical of himself, installed in his own internal state. The passionate individual tends to be blind to his passion, but he is always plagued by doubt and anguish, for his passion and the object of his passion remain beyond him.

Autonomy - Heteronomy   Passion makes the subject autonomous, since it constitutes an existential drive, a vector for his preoccupations and his actions, permeating throughout his daily life. Feelings make the subject dependent on external events or uncontrolled internal processes. Of course the emergence of a passion does not come out of a conscious and deliberate decision, but once the passion is present, it becomes the vector for one's existence, it provokes and maintains a certain continuity of being, an existential anchorage that can make the subject self-determined. When feelings do not provide such stability and continuity, since they are fleeting, inconsistent and rather accidental.

Well-being - Anxiety   Even though passion can imply a certain suffering, as the etymology of the words indicates, it grants a high level of psychological well-being, already because of its stability. It is connected to desire, it makes us strive for enjoyment, satisfaction and motivation, it provides us with energy by pursuing the goal that could make us happy. It gives us the power of trust and confidence. While feelings, because of their passive and unstable nature, tend to maintain a state of anxiety, a sentiment of anguishing uncertainty.

Authenticity - Sincerity   The passionate individual is authentic, he exposes what drives him fundamentally, he acts on the basis of his convictions, he is moved by his existential quest. When the feeling individual is sincere, he operates on the basis of immediate perceptions, his and others. His quest for comfort, his fear of uneasiness, his keen sensitivity make him respectful of psychological and social codes. He gives great credit to what he feels, so he expresses his beliefs and expects to be believed, as he does with others, he calls it sincerity. The passionate person is more ready to disturb those interpersonal rules, he is less attentive to his own feelings, less attentive to the emotional needs of his surroundings, he is more distant and critical with feeling states.

In spite of our criticism of the addiction or the glorification of feelings and emotions, we should not spurn those phenomena as uninteresting: they are central to the life-regulating processes, for man and almost all living creatures. Feelings can be characterized as mental experiences of body states, arising as the brain interprets emotions, themselves physical states arising from the body's responses to external stimuli. Most likely consciousness, whether the primitive process of animals or the reflexive self-conception of humans, requiring autobiographical memory, emerges from emotions and feelings. Clinical study actually showed that brain lesions impairing emotions inhibited decision making even though reason was unaffected. Those subjective perceptions can be thought of as the brain's mapping of body states for all living beings, although human language and reason use them further in a more specific way, since the intellect can develop from it a better understanding of the world. For example the experience of fear, anger or hunger, to the extent we establish a mental representation of them, present an access to reality. Mind begins at the level of feeling: it is when you have a feeling that you begin to have a mind, a self, a form of consciousness. But both our freedom and our understanding rely on our capacity for distance and critical analysis of these perceptions, making them an object of consciousness and reflection. We can therefore distinguish with Sartre both types of consciousness: pre-reflexive consciousness, primarily composed of feelings, emotions, impressions, and reflexive consciousness, constituted of concepts, explanations and analysis. In the first case we react to stimuli on a relatively immediate basis, in the second case we can decide to postpone, to ignore, to sublimate and even to refute those impressions, wherein lies our freedom and reason. And in spite of secondary cultural differences, for example with social emotions, there seems to be anthropological invariants and uniformity in emotional responses to diverse stimuli.

An interesting angle on the opposition between feelings and passion is addressed indirectly by an important distinction Augustine introduces between philocaly (love of beauty) and philosophy (love of wisdom or knowledge), following in this matter the platonic tradition. Philocaly refers to a love for beautiful things, possibly trivial, a mere feeling about pleasant objects, that can be converted into a love for authentic beautiful things, substantial beauty instead of superficial beauty, and finally this can be converted into the love for wisdom or philosophy through studying and working on oneself. There are three stages of love for beauty: immediate love for banal beauty, educated love for attested beautiful things, and love for beauty understood as wisdom, through the quest for some transcendent object or value. Augustine makes this accomplishment the subject of philosophical practice, or philosophy as a program for life. When we follow or obey our mere immediate feelings, we tend to remain in an initial emotional state, static, when passion represents a permanent drive for a "beyond"which implies a ceaseless and ruthless battle with oneself and the world. Nevertheless, philocaly is a necessary step, since it awakens in the soul the pleasure of perceiving beauty, an important cognitive and emotional relation to the world, to reality, to oneself: the joy of being.

In a way, the first step on the road to philosophy is a mere sentimentality, random and arbitrary. How then can we tie the encounter with philosophy with the unstable ground of the affects? Augustine views philocaly and philosophy as sisters born of the same father. "Although philocaly was dragged down from her heights by the birdlime of lust and kept in an ordinary cage, she retains the close resemblance of the ideal in her name (beauty), reminding the birdcatcher not to despise her. Her sister, flying freely, often sees her in a debased and needy condition with her wings clipped. Philocaly does not know from what origin she springs, only Philosophy knows that."The primary meaning of philocaly is purely aesthetic rather than moral, existential or ontological; it originally refers to the love of beauty in beautiful and precious things. It is an appreciation for something special, although the reasons why some objects are declared beautiful or precious are often not clearly defined. That is why the lover of beauty, in this original signification, is an amateur rather than a connoisseur, he is an "amateur of ornaments", of superficial trinkets. It is only through the work on oneself one can progress, but for this, the subject should learn not to be addicted to his feelings, he should learn not to blindly trust them or to adore them.

We could as well say that passion is a manifestation, an outpouring or a relic of our primordial, chaotic, unpredictable, enigmatic and primordial nature, which nevertheless remains our primary access to transcendence. Both permanent instability and ultimate stability. Each individual mind thus contains an inalienable part of the initial, cosmic and ontological abyss. A celestial parcel, and this inextinguishable spark pushes us and prompts us to surpass ourselves, causing tension, a desire to exist, an invitation to rejoin the ultimate and original nature from which it derives. A demon dwells in us, which torments us, which agitates our amorphous disposition, our inclination to tranquility, our forced quiescence, pushing us towards danger, excess, ecstasy, renunciation and even self-destruction. But for ordinary constitutions which are content with the mundane and the daily, this effervescent and uncontrollable factor remains somewhat ineffective; diluted and weakened; it is quickly absorbed and consumed by the inertia of habit and prudent routine. Those conventional persons will have had a certain experience of it, at specific times in their history, such as puberty, or the time of a romantic stir. Their soul will have briefly known this impetuosity, this intense agitation which shakes it, which expels it outside of itself, which propels it into ethereal spheres, tearing it away from the sadness and monotony of this lower world, so predictable, so common, so trite. Thus the average man more or less succeeds in extinguishing this flame which inhabits him, chloroforming it through the dictates of established morality, work, obligations, instinct for survival and established order. A psychological barrier is erected over time, which somehow manages to contain the wild course of passions. This one listens to the delightful delicacy of his feelings, we can call him the being of resentment, sadly and unconsciously unsatisfied.